FOOTBALL GROUNDS
FROM ABOVE

Above: the City Ground, home of Nottingham Forest, sited between the Notts County ground and the
Trent Bridge county cricket ground.

PHOTOGRAPHS BY

TEXT BY CASSANDRA WELLS

MYRIAD
LONDON

ARSENAL

Arsenal started out as a team called Dial Square in 1886, based in Woolwich, south-east London. They changed their name to Royal Arsenal in 1887, and to Woolwich Arsenal in 1891. Their early games were played on Woolwich Common, but they moved to Manor Field in 1888, where they remained for the next 26 years. Despite being successful in the league, which they joined in 1893, their gates were low, and they went into voluntary liquidation in 1910. Henry Norris, owner of Fulham FC bought the struggling club, and moved them to Highbury, north London, in 1913, much to the annoyance of their neighbours Spurs and Clapton Orient. After WWI Arsenal rejoined the first division, where they have remained since 1919. Architect Claude Waterlow Ferrier was charged with designing a stadium for Arsenal, and he set about using an art deco style for the ground. In 1931 he extended the terraces at each end, and began building the West Stand. The 1930s also saw success on the pitch; Arsenal won the League five times and the FA Cup twice. In 1935 an AFC monogrammed roof was added to the Laundry End terrace; in the same season a record attendance of 73,295 turned out to see Arsenal take on Sunderland. In 1936 the East Stand was replaced and looked almost identical to Ferrier's West Stand. The 1970s saw more seats installed at Highbury, and further developments came in the 1980s when the club added executive boxes to the Clock End. In 1991 the club drew up plans for a new North Stand in order to increase capacity. The club had to play in front of just three stands in the 1992-93 season as the bulldozers moved in and a mural took the place of the fans on the North Bank. The new two-tiered North Stand opened in 1993. The Clock End and the East and West terraces were next to be developed bringing a total capacity of 38,500 all-seated. In February 2004 Arsenal began building a 60,000 all-seater stadium just five minutes from Highbury at Ashburton Grove. At the beginning of the 2006-7 season Arsenal moved into the new Emirates Stadium. The new ground consists of a four-tier bowl with an all-seated capacity of 60,432.

Left: work in progress on the new Emirates Stadium at Ashburton Grove, with Highbury in the foreground

GROUND: **Emirates Stadium**
ADDRESS: **Highbury House, 75 Drayton Park, London N5 1BU**
MAIN TEL: **020 7704 4000**
BOX OFFICE: **020 7704 4040**
WEBSITE: **www.arsenal.com**
HOME COLOURS: **red shirts with white sleeves, white shorts with red trim, white and red hooped socks**
CLUB NICKNAME: **the Gunners**
CAPACITY: **60,432**
RECORD ATTENDANCE: **73,295 vs Sunderland, March 9 1935 (at Highbury)**
PITCH DIMENSIONS: **113m x 75m (123 x 82 yards)**
MOST PROLIFIC SCORER: **Thierry Henry (223 to January 20 2007)**
RECORD WIN: **12-0 vs Loughborough Town, March 12 1900**
RECORD DEFEAT: **0-8 vs Loughborough Town, December 8 1896**

ASTON VILLA

Aston Villa was formed by members of the Villa Cross Wesleyan Chapel in 1874. The club moved to the Aston Lower grounds in 1896 after spending 20 years at a basic ground on Wellington Road. The site was a leisure park dating back to the 1870s but had fallen into a state of disrepair. Villa began developing the ground, building a Main Stand on what had been a sub-tropical garden. Banking was raised on the other three sides of the ground and a basic barrel roof was added to the Trinity Road side. The ground opened in 1897, the same year Villa won the League and Cup double. Attendances continued to rise and prior to WWI and the club was drawing in regular crowds of 26,000. In 1914 Villa released their plans for future development of the ground. The work began with the removal of the concrete cycle path, which had run around the pitch; both end terraces were banked and another terrace added to the front of the Witton Lane Stand. After the war the Trinity Road stand was built, a structure which was so

extravagant in design that it cost the club £89,810. The Holte End was extended during WWII, and in 1946 Villa Park saw its highest ever crowd of 76,588. Villa Park's selection as a location for World Cup games brought about further developments with seats being added to the ground's terracing. A two-tiered North Stand was built in 1977, with further developments coming in light of the Taylor report. In 1990 the Holte End terracing was updated and the roof extended, but as a result of poor planning the whole structure had to be demolished in 1994 and replaced with a two-tier stand. Trinity Road Stand was refurbished in time for the 1996 European Cup. In order to maintain a capacity in excess of 40,000 the club set about planning to redevelop the Witton Lane Stand (now the Doug Ellis Stand), and by the end of 2002 the capacity was up to 42,632. There are plans for further development, filling in the corners of the North Stand to bring capacity up to 51,000.

GROUND: **Villa Park**
ADDRESS: **Villa Park, Trinity Road, Birmingham B6 6HE**
MAIN TEL: **0121 327 2299**
BOX OFFICE: **0121 327 5353**
WEBSITE: **www.avfc.co.uk**
CAPACITY: **42,584**
HOME COLOURS: **Claret shirts with blue trim, white shorts with claret and blue trim, blue socks with white turnover**
CLUB NICKNAMES: **The Villans, Villa**
PITCH DIMENSIONS: **105m x 65m (115 x 75 yards)**
FOUNDED: **1874**
RECORD ATTENDANCE: **76,588 vs Derby County March 2 1946**
MOST PROLIFIC SCORER: **Harry Hampton (215)**
RECORD WIN: **13-0 vs Wednesbury Old Athletic October 30 1886**
RECORD DEFEAT: **0-7 vs Blackburn Rovers October 19 1899**

BIRMINGHAM CITY

Birmingham City started out as the Small Heath Alliance in 1875. Their first pitch was on waste ground on Arthur Street, but as their crowd of followers grew, they moved to Muntz Street, where they remained for the next 29 years. The club turned professional in 1885, and changed their name to Birmingham FC in 1905. The Blues moved to St Andrews in 1906, onto a ground that had been previously occupied by gypsies, who are said to have laid a curse on it. A massive Main Stand was built, and in order to raise the height of the ground beneath terracing on the Coventry Road End, locals were encouraged to dump rubbish on the site. The Kop terrace was built on top, with a capacity of 48,000. Terrace covers were put on top of the Railway End and the Kop by the time the ground recorded its highest gate ever of 67,341 in 1939. During WWII the curse returned and as well as being bombed 20 times, the Main Stand burned down when a fireman inadvertently used petrol instead of water to put out a brazier. Birmingham had to move to Leamington and then Villa Park until 1943 while their ground was repaired. They came out of the war with a new name, Birmingham City FC. The Kop reopened in 1947 and a new two-tiered Main stand opened in 1954. Success in Europe funded the building of the Railway End Stand in 1963-4. The 1980s saw a run of bad luck, and by 1989 the Blues found themselves in the third division. March 1993 saw the Blues' fortunes improve as David Sullivan took over ownership of the club. Sullivan laid out plans for a £4.5million development of the Kop and Tilton Road End, which opened in 1994. The Railway End was redeveloped in 1999, and there are plans to develop the Main Stand sometime in the future.

GROUND: **St Andrews**
ADDRESS: St Andrews, Birmingham B9 4NH
MAIN TEL: 0121 772 0101
BOX OFFICE: 0906 833 2988
WEBSITE: www.bcfc.com
CAPACITY: 30,009
HOME COLOURS: Blue shirts, blue shorts, blue and white socks
CLUB NICKNAME: The Blues
PITCH DIMENSIONS: 101m x 67m (110 x 73 yards)
FOUNDED: 1875
RECORD ATTENDANCE: 66,844 vs Everton February 11 1939
MOST PROLIFIC SCORER: Joe Bradford (249)
RECORD WIN: 12-0 vs Walsall T. Swifts December 17 1892
RECORD DEFEAT: 1-9 vs Sheffield Wednesday December 13 1930

BLACKBURN ROVERS

Blackburn Rovers were formed in 1875 by a group of former public schoolboys. It took them a year before they settled at their first ground – Oozehead – to play regular matches. They moved a further four times before settling at Ewood Park in 1890. During this time they had become the first real giants of English football, winning the FA Cup three years in a row from 1884 and again in 1890. In 1905 Laurence Cotton, a textile baron, went about transforming the ground in a way Jack Walker would almost 90 years later. Between 1905-1914 he spent an estimated £12,000 on players and £33,000 on ground improvements. First came a pitched roof on the Darwen End, followed by the building of the Main Stand and the Nuttall Street Stand. Further improvements in 1914 came after Rovers had won the League title, when the Riverside Stand was built. By 1913 the capacity was 70,866.

Not a lot changed at the ground until 1960, when a Cup Final appearance helped to fund a cantilevered roof over the Blackburn End. In 1980 safety regulations brought the capacity at Ewood Park down to 23,400 and tough times followed. In 1983 just 3,797 turned up to see the last game of the season. Fire checks in 1985 saw the upper tier of the Riverside End closed and the terrace below closed. In 1987 Rovers' fortunes improved and Chairman Bill Fox convinced his friend, Jack Walker, to help build a new Riverside Stand. This would be the start of a remarkable relationship. In 1991 Walker decided to buy a 62 per cent share in the club, and spent £13m on the team in his first 18 months. He then laid out plans for the building of three two-tiered stands. The building work incensed some locals, as houses and a local mill would need to be demolished. Regardless of this, the council approved the plans and in 1993 the developments began. When the Jack Walker Stand was opened in November 1994, the capacity was up to 31,367.

GROUND: **Ewood Park**
ADDRESS: Ewood Park, Blackburn, Lancashire BB2 4JF
MAIN TEL: 01254 698 888
BOX OFFICE: 08701 123456
WEBSITE: www.rovers.co.uk
CAPACITY: 31,367
HOME COLOURS: Blue and white halved shirts, white shorts with a blue trim, white socks with blue trim
CLUB NICKNAME: Rovers
PITCH DIMENSIONS: 105m x 66m (115 x 72 yards)
FOUNDED: 1875
RECORD ATTENDANCE: 62,522 vs Bolton Wanderers March 2 1929
MOST PROLIFIC SCORER: Simon Gurner (168)
RECORD WIN: 11-0 vs Rossendale October 13 1884
RECORD DEFEAT: 0-8 vs Arsenal February 25 1933

BOLTON WANDERERS

Bolton Wanderers started out as a Sunday school team called Christ Church FC, playing on Park Recreation Ground. They moved to Dick Cockle's Field on Pikes Lane in 1877, where the club had a row with the vicar and left to become Bolton Wanderers. In 1881 they moved to a proper sports ground on Pikes Lane, which had two small stands. In 1893 rising rents led Wanderers to bid farewell to Pikes Lane and build a new ground on wasteland. That ground, Burnden Park, would remain home to the Trotters for 102 years. Wanderers were one of the 12 founding members of the Football League, although the league title is one they have never won. Their success has always been with the FA Cup, a prize they have won four times, the last time being in 1958 when Trotters legend Nat Lofthouse scored both of Bolton's goals against Manchester United. Their first attempt at winning the Cup came in 1904 however, and despite losing the final, the money raised meant they could build a main stand and terrace and cover the Great Lever End. The 1920s saw three FA Cup wins for Bolton, and again more ground improvements followed with the new Burnden Stand being built. Not much changed at the ground for the following 70 years. The 1980s were the next major period of change for the club, as their fortunes had faded, and the club had sunk from the first division to the fourth. Crowds dropped to an all time low of 2,902 and, to raise revenue, the Trotters sold some of their land at the Railway End to a local superstore. By the 1990s, Bolton's fortunes had reversed; they reached the Premiership in 1995 and made plans for a 28,700 all-seater stadium. The impressive Reebok stadium opened in 1997, the same season Colin Todd took Wanderers back to the Premiership.

GROUND: **Reebok Stadium**
ADDRESS: **Burnden Way, Lostock, Bolton BL6 6JW**
MAIN TEL: **01204 673 673**
BOX OFFICE: **0871 871 2932**
WEBSITE: **www.bwfc.co.uk**
CAPACITY: **28,723**
HOME COLOURS: **White shirts, navy shorts, navy socks**
CLUB NICKNAME: **The Trotters**
PITCH DIMENSIONS: **101m x 64m (114 x 74 yards)**
FOUNDED: **1874**
RECORD ATTENDANCE: **69,912 vs Manchester City February 18 1933**
MOST PROLIFIC SCORER: **Nat Lofthouse (255)**
RECORD WIN: **13-0 vs Sheffield United February 1 1890**
RECORD DEFEAT: **1-9 vs Preston North End December 12 1887**

CARDIFF CITY

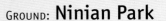

Cardiff City emerged from Riverside FC, a team formed in 1899 from players at the Riverside Cricket Club. Ninian Park was then a rubbish tip between Sloper Road and the Taff Vale railway line. When they turned professional in 1909, the club bought a seven year lease on the ground, and before their first game against Aston Villa the players still had to clear debris from the pitch. The ground was fairly basic, with a small wooden grandstand on the Sloper Road side. The team won promotion in their first season in the League, finished runners up in the First Division in 1924 and in 1927 they won the FA Cup. During this successful period the club built the Canton Stand at the north end and following their FA Cup success, they built a roof over the Grangetown End terrace. A bad run of form followed, and when in 1937 the Main Stand burned down, Cardiff were languishing in division three. By 1952 they were back in the First Division and gates were averaging 38,000. Despite being relegated again, the club continued to develop the ground and by 1960 they were back in the top flight. The ground was frequently used for Welsh internationals – 51 in total between 1946-76. The Safety of Sports Grounds Act in 1977 saw the capacity at Ninian Park slashed to 10,000 while it was repaired. The Grangetown End roof was demolished and the banking was cut down. Bad performances on the pitch coupled with boardroom bickering saw Cardiff hit an all time low in 1991 when just 1,629 fans saw them defeated by Aldershot, and they almost went into liquidation. They were saved by millionaire holiday resort owner Rick Wright, who ploughed £2m into the club. In 1991 more seats were installed in the Main Stand, the Bob Bank and the Canton Stand, and the Grangemouth End was restored. Sam Hamman bought the club in 2000 and has been investing heavily; by the end of the 2004 season the capacity was up to 20,000.

GROUND: **Ninian Park**
ADDRESS: **Ninian Park, Sloper Road, Cardiff, CF11 8SX**
MAIN TEL: **029 2022 1001**
BOX OFFICE: **0845 345 1400**
WEBSITE: **www.cardiffcity.co.uk**
CAPACITY: **21,500**
HOME COLOURS: **Blue shirts, white shorts, white socks**
CLUB NICKNAME: **The Bluebirds**
PITCH DIMENSIONS: **101m x 69m (110 x 75 yards)**
FOUNDED: **1899**
RECORD ATTENDANCE: **57,893 vs Arsenal April 22 1953**
MOST PROLIFIC SCORER: **Len Davies (128)**
RECORD WIN: **8-0 vs Enfield November 28 1931**
RECORD DEFEAT: **2-11 vs Sheffield United January 1 1926**

CELTIC

Celtic was formed in 1888 as a charitable trust for the Catholic communities in Glasgow's East End. They played games at a ground called Celtic Park from 1888 until 1892. When they could no longer afford the rent, they moved to a former brickyard in Parkhead, and named it too Celtic Park. The club quickly built a grandstand and a pavilion with terracing on both ends. In 1898 the club's director, James Grant, paid for the Grant Stand to be built; it was unusual in that it was on stilts, had padded seats and windows along the front and side. The Grant Stand was demolished in 1929 and a South Stand built in its place. By 1938 Celtic Park recorded its largest ever crowd of 92,000 in an Old Firm clash with Rangers. The next major changes to the ground took place between 1957-71, reflecting the success the Bhoys were having on the pitch. The Rangers End was covered following Celtic's European Cup triumph in 1967. In 1986 the club added a new front to the South Stand in readiness for the club's centenary; however Celtic's reluctance to add more seats cost them dear in the aftermath of the Hillsborough disaster. Celtic's debts were high, and a plan was announced to move the club to a new 52,000 all-seater stadium. The fans weren't keen and began boycotting games. As debts soared, the club faced receivership until Fergus McCann, a Canadian businessman took over the club. He ditched the planned move and began developing Celtic Park into an all-seater stadium. Now the ground is fully enclosed, with three new two-tier stands and the older Main Stand bringing the capacity up to 60,832.

GROUND: **Celtic Park**
ADDRESS: **Celtic Park, Glasgow G40 3RE**
MAIN TEL: **0141 556 2611**
BOX OFFICE: **0141 551 8653**
WEBSITE: **www.celticfc.net**
CAPACITY: **60,506**
HOME COLOURS: **Emerald green and white hooped shirts, white shorts with green trim, white socks**
CLUB NICKNAME: **The Bhoys**
PITCH DIMENSIONS: **110m x 68m (120 x 74 yards)**
FOUNDED: **1888**
RECORD ATTENDANCE: **92,000 vs Rangers January 1, 1938**
MOST PROLIFIC SCORER: **James McGrory (397)**
RECORD WIN: **11-0 vs Dundee October 10 1895**
RECORD DEFEAT: **0-8 vs Motherwell April 30 1937**

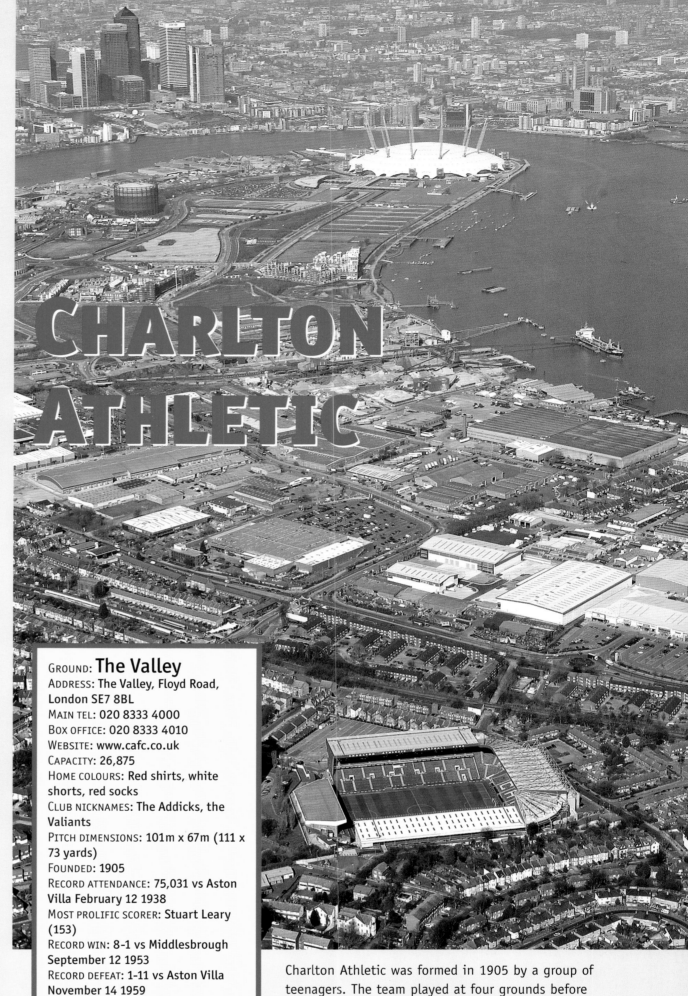

CHARLTON ATHLETIC

GROUND: **The Valley**
ADDRESS: **The Valley, Floyd Road, London SE7 8BL**
MAIN TEL: **020 8333 4000**
BOX OFFICE: **020 8333 4010**
WEBSITE: **www.cafc.co.uk**
CAPACITY: **26,875**
HOME COLOURS: **Red shirts, white shorts, red socks**
CLUB NICKNAMES: **The Addicks, the Valiants**
PITCH DIMENSIONS: **101m x 67m (111 x 73 yards)**
FOUNDED: **1905**
RECORD ATTENDANCE: **75,031 vs Aston Villa February 12 1938**
MOST PROLIFIC SCORER: **Stuart Leary (153)**
RECORD WIN: **8-1 vs Middlesbrough September 12 1953**
RECORD DEFEAT: **1-11 vs Aston Villa November 14 1959**

Charlton Athletic was formed in 1905 by a group of teenagers. The team played at four grounds before arriving at the Valley in 1919. At the time the Valley was a chalk and sand pit known as "the swamp". Volunteers helped to dig out a pitch and banking was formed at either end. By 1921, when the club had turned professional and built the Main Stand on the west side of the pitch, the ground was famed for its vast East Terrace. In 1923 the club decided to leave the Valley and move to a ground called The Mount. Charlton moved back to the Valley after just one season. The club had run up huge debts and were facing a bleak future until the Gliksten brothers stepped in with a £100,000 rescue package in 1931. Success on the pitch under the management of Jimmy Seed saw the fan base swell and in 1938 the Valley recorded its highest ever gate of 75,031. Despite winning the FA Cup in 1947, the club didn't carry out any further developments until 1950 when a few hundred seats were added to the Main Stand paddock. In the 1980s, the club announced plans to make the ground all-seater. However, bad financial decisions meant Charlton had to leave the Valley in 1985, and moved in with local rivals Crystal Palace. New directors and a massive campaign by the club's dedicated fans led to an announcement in 1989 that Charlton would be moving back to the Valley. Fans and directors alike helped clear the overgrown Valley, but in 1990 Greenwich Council turned down the plans. After forming a political party, the fans finally achieved their goal and despite having to spend a further season at Upton Park, the club moved back to the Valley in 1992. Since then the ground has been totally redeveloped with a large single tiered East Stand, a two-tiered North and West Stand and the Jimmy Seed Stand, which remains a small single-tiered structure. The north-east and north-west corners have been filled in, and there are plans for the redevelopment of the Jimmy Seed Stand to bring capacity up to 35,000.

CHELSEA

Chelsea was formed in 1905, but the club's ground, Stamford Bridge, came into being almost 30 years earlier in 1877, when the London Athletic Club developed it as a running track from an orchard and market garden. In 1904 Gus Mears took over the ownership of the ground and developed it into a venue for cycling, athletics and football. Mears contracted Scottish architect, Archibald Leith, to design the main stand, a 5,000-seater construction. Mears and his friend Fred Parker established Chelsea FC in 1905. Chelsea had a remarkably successful first season and by 1907 their promotion to the First Division saw them attracting the highest gates in the League. Despite staging FA Cup finals and other sporting events, the cub did not invest much money in the ground. It wasn't until 1935 that a cover was added to the Fulham Road terrace. This was the same year the club recorded its highest ever gate of 82,905 in a game against Arsenal. In 1939 a 2,500-seat stand was erected on the north-east corner, on stilts above the terracing. A new North Stand was opened in 1945, but it was the 1960s and 1970s when the major developments took place at the Bridge. At the time the West Stand was built, the team were going through one of their most successful periods ever, winning the League Cup in 1965 and the FA Cup in 1970. They also won the European Cup Winners' Cup in 1971. In that year plans were laid down for a three-tier East Stand, the first stand in the £5.5m development. The Stand opened in 1974, but Chelsea's luck took a turn for the worse. They were heavily in debt, they were relegated to the Second Division and gates were dropping. In the 1982-83 season gates twice dropped to below 7,000. This was the season in which Ken Bates took over as chairman. Over the following 20 years, Chelsea Village was developed. Two new all seat stands were built at each end and corner stands were added. In 2001 the West Stand was rebuilt, a two-tiered stand bringing the capacity up to 42,449.

GROUND: **Stamford Bridge**
ADDRESS: **Stamford Bridge, London SW6 1HS**
MAIN TEL: 020 7385 5545
BOX OFFICE: 0870 300 1212
WEBSITE: www.chelseafc.com
CAPACITY: 42,449
HOME COLOURS: **Royal blue shirts with white and amber trim, royal blue shorts with white and blue trim, white socks with blue and amber trim**
CLUB NICKNAME: **The Blues**
PITCH DIMENSIONS: **103m x 68m (113 x 74 yards)**
FOUNDED: **1905**
RECORD ATTENDANCE: **82,905 vs Arsenal October 12 1935**
MOST PROLIFIC SCORER: **Bobby Tambling (164)**
RECORD WIN: **13-0 vs Jeunesse Hautcharage September 29 1971**
RECORD DEFEAT: **1-8 vs Wolverhampton Wanderers December 26 1953**

CRYSTAL PALACE

Crystal Palace was formed in 1905, when the club took up residency at the Crystal Palace ground, which was then England's national stadium. In 1915 the team moved on to the Herne Hill cycle and athletics ground as the Admiralty took over the ground. In 1918 Palace moved to the Nest, a ground situated opposite Selhurst station. In 1919 Crystal Palace paid £2,570 for a former brickfield, Selhurst Park. It took a further five years for the site to be prepared. The club's plans for development were fairly conservative, with one stand and minimal terracing. The Main Stand was built to a similar design to those at Chelsea and Fulham. A healthy rise in gates followed its opening, despite the club being relegated. In the 1950s the ground fell into a state of disrepair as the Eagles languished in the third and fourth divisions. The 1960s were more successful. Following the installation of floodlights in 1962, chairman Arthur Wait persuaded Real Madrid to play a friendly at Selhurst Park. The uncovered Park Side was developed in 1969 into a stand with a 42m deep shed-like roof covering the original banking. In 1979 a record 51,482 saw Palace win the second division championship. Palace spent the next 12 seasons yo-yoing between the first and third divisions. The 1980s also signalled the first ever long-term ground sharing plans at Selhurst Park, firstly with local rivals Charlton Athletic and then with Wimbledon. The 1990s saw more major development: the Arthur Wait stand was converted to an all-seater, a hospitality block was built behind the main stand and the development of the White Horse Lane end brought the capacity up to 30,115. The most major development, however, came at the Holmesdale End stand. Built into a natural embankment and surrounded by houses, development was always going to be difficult, however, structural engineers worked their magic and a massive structure, which took more than a year to build, was finally opened in August 1995, raising the capacity to 24,600.

GROUND: Selhurst Park
ADDRESS: Selhurst Park, South Norwood, London SE25 6PU
MAIN TEL: 020 8768 6000
BOX OFFICE: 020 8771 8841
WEBSITE: www.cpfc.co.uk
CAPACITY: 26,400
HOME COLOURS: Red and blue striped shirts, red shorts, red socks with blue tops
CLUB NICKNAMES: The Eagles, Palace
PITCH DIMENSIONS: 101m x 68m (110 x 74 yards)
FOUNDED: 1905
RECORD ATTENDANCE: 51,482 vs Burnley May 11 1979
MOST PROLIFIC SCORER: Peter Simpson (153)
RECORD WIN: 9-0 vs Barrow October 11 1959
RECORD DEFEAT: 0-9 vs Burnley February 10 1909

DERBY COUNTY

Players from Derby County Cricket Club formed Derby County FC in 1884. Their first pitch was part of the cricket ground, which was in the middle of a racecourse. Derby quickly tired of rescheduling games that clashed with race meetings and, in 1895, they moved to a baseball ground that owner Francis Ley had built after a visit to the US. The Baseball Ground, as the stadium became known, was very enclosed however, and in 1923 Derby received an offer to move to Osmanton Park stadium. They turned this offer down and in 1924 they bought the Baseball Ground from Francis Ley. In 1925 the Popular Side was concreted, a year later the Rams went back up to division one, which funded further ground developments. A two-tiered stand was built where the Osmanton Terrace and Catcher's Corner had stood, which opened in 1933. By the start of WWII all four sides of the Baseball Ground had been rebuilt and covered. The Rams returned to the first division in 1969 under the management of Brian Clough; this was the same year the Ley Stand opened, and a record 41,826 fans crammed in to see Derby take on Spurs. Crowd trouble in the late 1970s and 1980s saw fences and bars erected throughout the ground, and calls by local residents for the club to move. The 1980s also saw massive debts for Derby County and relegation to the third division. These problems were eased when Robert Maxwell took over as chairman in 1984. The fences came down in 1989 and after the Taylor report, the club put together plans for rebuilding the stadium. The club were offered another chance to move from the ground, this time to Pride Park. Yet again they turned the offer down and began working on plans for a 28,000 all-seater Baseball Ground. However, in 1995, after seeing the success of Middlesbrough's relocation they reassessed their plans and took up the offer of a move to Pride Park. The £16m project took 46 weeks to complete, and at the start of the 1997/98 season the Rams began playing at Pride Park, a 33,258 all-seater stadium.

GROUND: **Pride Park Stadium**
ADDRESS: **Pride Park Stadium, Derby DE24 8XL**
MAIN TEL: 01332 202 202
BOX OFFICE: 01332 209 209
WEBSITE: www.dcfc.co.uk
CAPACITY: 33,597
HOME COLOURS: White shirts with black trim, black shorts with white trim, white socks
CLUB NICKNAME: The Rams
PITCH DIMENSIONS: 101m x 68m (110 x 74 yards)
FOUNDED: 1884
RECORD ATTENDANCE: 41,826 vs Tottenham Hotspur September 20 1969
MOST PROLIFIC SCORER: Steve Bloomer (292)
RECORD WIN: 9-0 vs Wolverhampton Wanderers January 10 1891
RECORD DEFEAT: 2-11 vs Everton January 18 1889

EVERTON

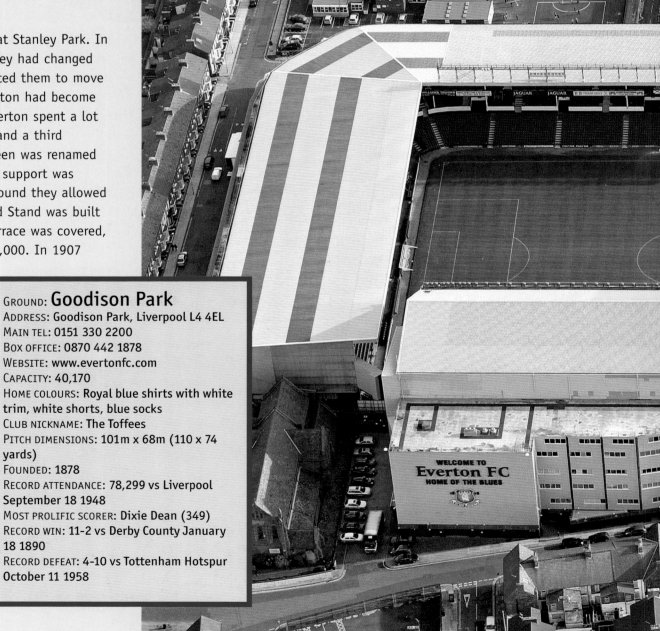

Everton started out as St Domingo's FC in 1878, playing games at Stanley Park. In 1884 they became the first tenants at Anfield, by which time they had changed their name to Everton. A row with their landlord in 1892 prompted them to move to Goodison Park, then called Mere Green. During that time Everton had become founder members of the League in 1888, winning it in 1891. Everton spent a lot of money preparing the ground, building two uncovered stands and a third covered stand with seating, as well as fixing the pitch. Mere Green was renamed Goodison Park in time for its official opening in 1892. Everton's support was unrivalled at the time, and the FA was so impressed with the ground they allowed the 1894 Cup Final to be played there. In 1895 the Bullens Road Stand was built following the ground's first international. The Goodison Road terrace was covered, and by 1905 the ground was estimated to have a capacity of 55,000. In 1907 Scottish engineer Archibald Leitch built the two-tiered Park End stand at Goodison, before building a magnificent Main Stand in 1909, which had a pitched roof and central gable. It wasn't until 1926 that the ground saw any more improvements, when a two-tiered stand was built on the Bullens Road side. Twelve years later this was linked to the Gladwys Street end, making Goodison Park the first to have two-tiered stands on all sides. In 1948 the ground saw a record 78,299 fans cram in for a Merseyside derby against Liverpool. The 1970s saw a new three-tier Main Stand replace Leitch's original and a new roof on the Bullen's Road Stand, which was brought round to cover the Gladwys Street end in 1986. In the aftermath of the Taylor report, seats were added to the remaining terraces, and in 1994 a new single-tier Park End Stand was built. There is now talk that the club will move to a new 55,000 purpose-built stadium at Central Docks, as Goodison Park's capacity remains at 40,170.

GROUND: **Goodison Park**
ADDRESS: **Goodison Park, Liverpool L4 4EL**
MAIN TEL: 0151 330 2200
BOX OFFICE: 0870 442 1878
WEBSITE: www.evertonfc.com
CAPACITY: 40,170
HOME COLOURS: Royal blue shirts with white trim, white shorts, blue socks
CLUB NICKNAME: The Toffees
PITCH DIMENSIONS: 101m x 68m (110 x 74 yards)
FOUNDED: 1878
RECORD ATTENDANCE: 78,299 vs Liverpool September 18 1948
MOST PROLIFIC SCORER: Dixie Dean (349)
RECORD WIN: 11-2 vs Derby County January 18 1890
RECORD DEFEAT: 4-10 vs Tottenham Hotspur October 11 1958

FULHAM

Fulham started out as Fulham St Andrews, a church team, in 1879. They moved grounds eight times before they finally arrived at Craven Cottage in 1896. The original Craven Cottage, which burnt down in 1888, was built in 1789 by Baron Craven. The team turned professional in 1898, and by 1905 they were drawing crowds in the region of 20,000, more than their neighbours at Chelsea. The club spent £15,000 developing the ground; this included three terraces and a corner pavilion, the Cottage. The only stand to be built was on Stevenage Road, which had an upper tier of seats, a paddock in front covered by a pitched roof and gable in the centre. It was not until the 1960s that further developments took place. In 1961 the Hammersmith End was extended and in 1965 it was covered. The Riverside terrace was replaced by the Riverside Stand in 1971, although the cost of this stand almost bankrupted the club. For the next 20 years Fulham fell into decline, gates dropped and debts stacked up. In the early 1990s the club's future at Craven Cottage looked very doubtful as property developers took over ownership of the ground. In 1991 Fulham started ground sharing talks with Chelsea, although these never came to anything. Perhaps Fulham's lowest moment came in January 1996 when they were second bottom of the third division, drawing crowds of around 4,000 and facing an exit from the League. However, their fortunes changed completely on May 29 1997 when Harrod's owner Mohammed Al Fayed took over ownership of the club. He brought with him a five-year plan to get the club into the Premiership. He spent millions on players and in just four years this dream was realised. He then went about redeveloping the ground. In 2002 Fulham left Craven Cottage to ground share at QPR's Loftus Road. Again rumours started that Al Fayed was going to sell the ground; however these proved unfounded and at the start of the 2004-5 season the Cottagers moved back to Craven Cottage, to a state of the art stadium, capable of holding 30,000 fans.

GROUND: **Craven Cottage**
ADDRESS: Craven Cottage, Stevenage Road, Fulham, London SW6 6HH
MAIN TEL: 020 7893 8383
BOX OFFICE: 0870 442 1234
WEBSITE: www.fulhamfc.com
CAPACITY: 30,000
HOME COLOURS: White shirts with black and red trim, black shorts, white socks with red and black trim
CLUB NICKNAMES: The Cottagers, the Whites
PITCH DIMENSIONS: 102m x 66m (112 x 72 yards)
FOUNDED: 1879
RECORD ATTENDANCE: 49,335 vs Millwall October 8 1938
MOST PROLIFIC SCORER: Gordon Davies (159)
RECORD WIN: 10-1 vs Ipswich December 26 1963
RECORD DEFEAT: 0-10 vs Liverpool September 23 1986

HAMPDEN PARK (QUEEN'S PARK)

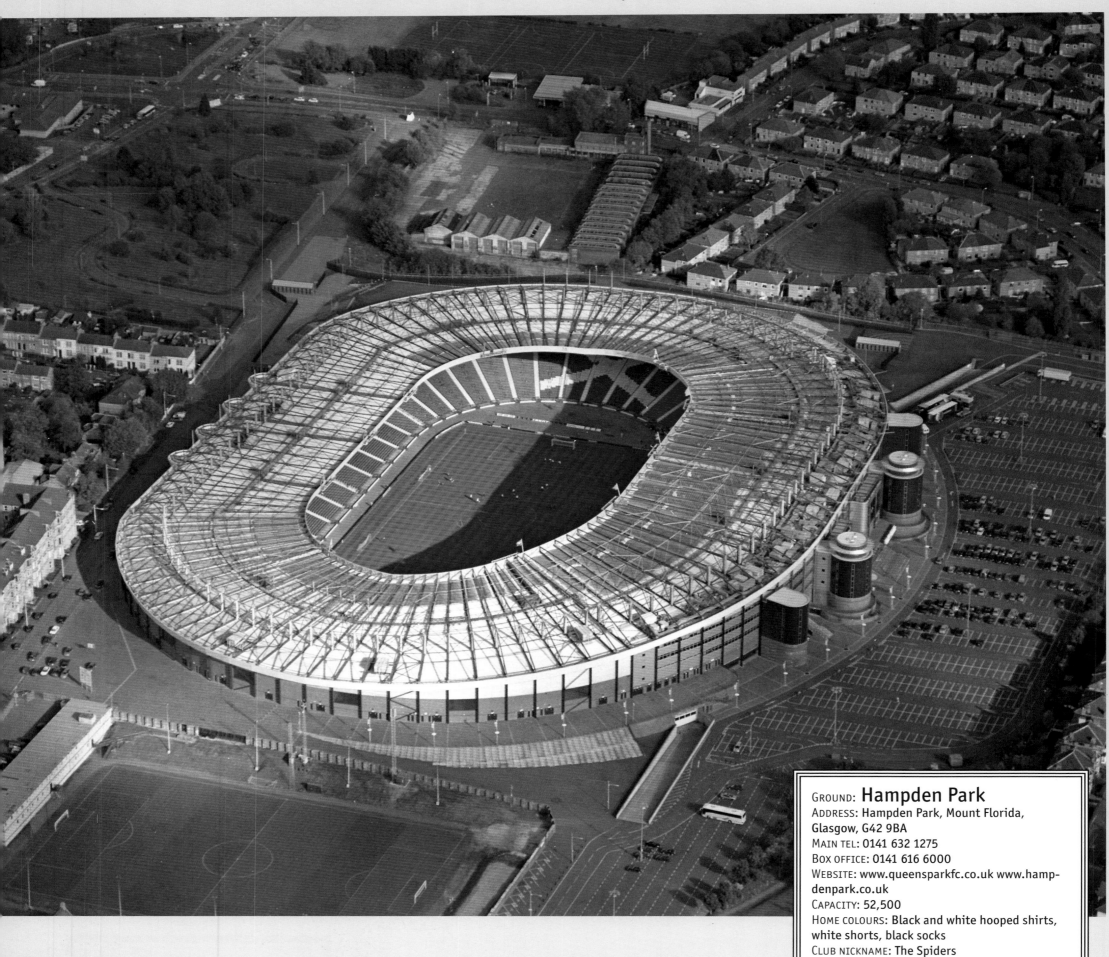

GROUND: **Hampden Park**
ADDRESS: **Hampden Park, Mount Florida, Glasgow, G42 9BA**
MAIN TEL: **0141 632 1275**
BOX OFFICE: **0141 616 6000**
WEBSITE: **www.queensparkfc.co.uk www.hampdenpark.co.uk**
CAPACITY: **52,500**
HOME COLOURS: **Black and white hooped shirts, white shorts, black socks**
CLUB NICKNAME: **The Spiders**
PITCH DIMENSIONS: **105m x 69m (115 x 75 yards)**
FOUNDED: **1867**
RECORD ATTENDANCE: **95,772 vs Rangers January 12 1929**
MOST PROLIFIC SCORER: **James McAlpine (163)**
RECORD WIN: **16-0 vs St Peter's August 29 1885**
RECORD DEFEAT: **0-9 vs Motherwell April 29 1930**

Queen's Park is Scotland's oldest football club, dating back to 1867. The club played early games at Queen's Park Recreation Ground before moving to their own ground, the first Hampden Park, on Queen's Drive in 1873. They moved to Titwood Park in 1883, before arriving at the second Hampden Park in 1884. It wasn't long before the ground was being used for Cup Finals. The club moved again in 1903 to a yet larger site, the third Hampden Park, which had a capacity of 65,000. Scottish architect Archibald Leith designed the ground's two stands on the south side with a pavilion in between and an oval bowl of terracing around the rest of the ground. The club continued to do well, finishing fifth in Division One in 1929. Further developments took place in the 1930s when the North Stand was built at the back of the Main Stand terracing, bringing the capacity up to 150,000. This led to the ground being used for internationals and in 1937 the highest crowd ever to attend a football game – 149,415 fans – packed in to see Scotland play England. Until the 1950s Hampden Park was the largest ground in the world. In the 1960s a roof was added to the West Stand, but the club lacked funds to carry out more major, and necessary, refurbishments.

During the 1970s Hampden Park's future hung in the balance as the Scottish Football Association tried to decide how the renovations would be funded.

By 1981 an appeal had raised the necessary funds to begin redeveloping Hampden Park. The North Stand was demolished and concrete added to the terraces. The next phase was delayed as the Taylor report meant developments were going to be more costly and key thinkers began to question whether it was cost-effective to renovate the ground seeing as Ibrox and Murrayfield were so close by. However, eventually the decision came to develop Hampden Park and in 1992 work began. Seats and roofs were added to the North and East stands, and now the ground has a 52,500 all-seater capacity. Queen's Park remains the only amateur football club still in the Scottish Football League.

HEART OF MIDLOTHIAN

Heart of Midlothian FC formed in 1874, taking their name from a dance club in Edinburgh. They started out playing games on the East Meadows and Powderhall grounds before moving to Gorgie Road in 1881. They moved from the first Tynecastle Park across the road to the current Tynecastle Park in 1886. Hearts was a founder member of the Scottish Football League in 1890. The ground had a pavilion, a stand and a cycle track installed in 1903. By 1914 Hearts had won two league titles and four Cup Finals and they began building a Main Stand. This came complete with an owl on top to frighten off other birds from the ground. In 1926 the club bought the ground and began building up the terraces, although its location between narrow streets, a school and the North British Distillery meant expansion was going to be very difficult. When a record 53,396 fans crammed in for a Cup tie with Rangers the club seriously thought about relocating to Murrayfield; however, WWII put paid to this plan. The 1950s and '60s saw further successes on the pitch, Hearts won the League twice, the League Cup four times and the Scottish Cup once, all of which helped to fund the concreting of the terraces, and a roof on the Wheatfield Street side. Further developments came in the wake of the Safety of Sports Ground Act in the 1970s. Hearts' chairman, Walter Mercer, ploughed £500,000 into developing the ground, adding benches beneath the Wheatfield Street cover and seats to the Main Stand paddock. The Taylor report led Hearts to consider leaving Tynecastle Park as capacity was so limited. In the end, the club decided to redevelop Tynecastle Park. Two all-seater stands were built on the north and west sides in the mid 1990s, followed by a new stand on the south side. The club's financial worries continue to haunt them and there are still plans for the club to move to Murrayfield if their finances do not improve.

GROUND: **Tynecastle Park**
ADDRESS: **Tynecastle Park, Gorgie Road, Edinburgh EH11 2HL**
MAIN TEL: **0131 200 7200**
BOX OFFICE: **0131 200 7201**
WEBSITE: **www.heartsfc.co.uk**
CAPACITY: **18,008**
HOME COLOURS: **Maroon shirts with white trim, white shorts with maroon trim, maroon socks**
CLUB NICKNAME: **Hearts, the Jam Tarts**
PITCH DIMENSIONS: **98m x 68m (107 x 74 yards)**
FOUNDED: **1874**
RECORD ATTENDANCE: **53,396**
MOST PROLIFIC SCORER: **John Robertson (208)**
RECORD WIN: **10-3 vs Queens Park August 24 1912**
RECORD DEFEAT: **0-7 vs Hibernian January 1 1973**

HIBERNIAN

Hibernian was formed in 1875 by a group of Irish football enthusiasts. They called the team Hibernian after the Latin name for Ireland. They shared their early grounds with Hearts. They moved three times before arriving at the first Easter Road in 1880, not far from the present ground. In 1891 Hibs disbanded after many of their players left to play for Celtic and developers took over the ground. Two years later they reformed and found themselves a ground not far from the original Easter Road, which opened in February 1893. Success followed and Hibs won their first league title in 1903. There was talk of the club moving again, but in 1922 they signed a 25-year lease on Easter Road. Developments began in 1924, when the pitch was moved sideways, raised banking was built on three sides and a stand on the west side. After WWII, Easter Road recorded its highest ever attendance of 65,480 for a game against Hearts in 1950, and the East Terrace was extended not long afterwards. The North Terrace was covered in the 1960s, but no further developments came until the 1980s. Easter Road was the first Scottish club to instal undersoil heating in 1980; two years later benches were added to the North Stand, and in 1985 the height of the East Terrace was reduced. Hibs were floated on the Stock Exchange, but a disastrous business plan saw the club almost merged with Hearts to form Edinburgh United. However protests from the fans and investment from chairman David Duff saw off the idea. The Taylor report meant the club had to consider either moving or further developing Easter Road. Plans to move four miles away to a 20,000 all-seater ground in Straiton were shelved in 1994 following fierce opposition from fans, so Easter Road had to be quickly developed. Two new stands were built at either end and in 2001 a double-decker stand opened on the west side. Seats have been added to the old East Terrace and capacity is now 17,500.

GROUND: **Easter Road Stadium**
ADDRESS: **Easter Road Stadium, 12 Albion Place, Edinburgh EH7 5QG**
MAIN TEL: **0131 661 2159**
BOX OFFICE: **0131 661 1875**
WEBSITE: **www.hibs.org.uk**
CAPACITY: **17,500**
HOME COLOURS: **Green and white shirts, white shorts, green socks with white trim**
CLUB NICKNAME: **The Hibees**
PITCH DIMENSIONS: **102m x 68m (112 x 74 yards)**
FOUNDED: **1875**
RECORD ATTENDANCE: **65,860 vs Hearts January 2 1950**
MOST PROLIFIC SCORER: **Gordon Smith (364)**
RECORD WIN: **22-1 vs 42nd Highlanders September 3 1881**
RECORD DEFEAT: **0-6 vs Celtic October 15 1960**

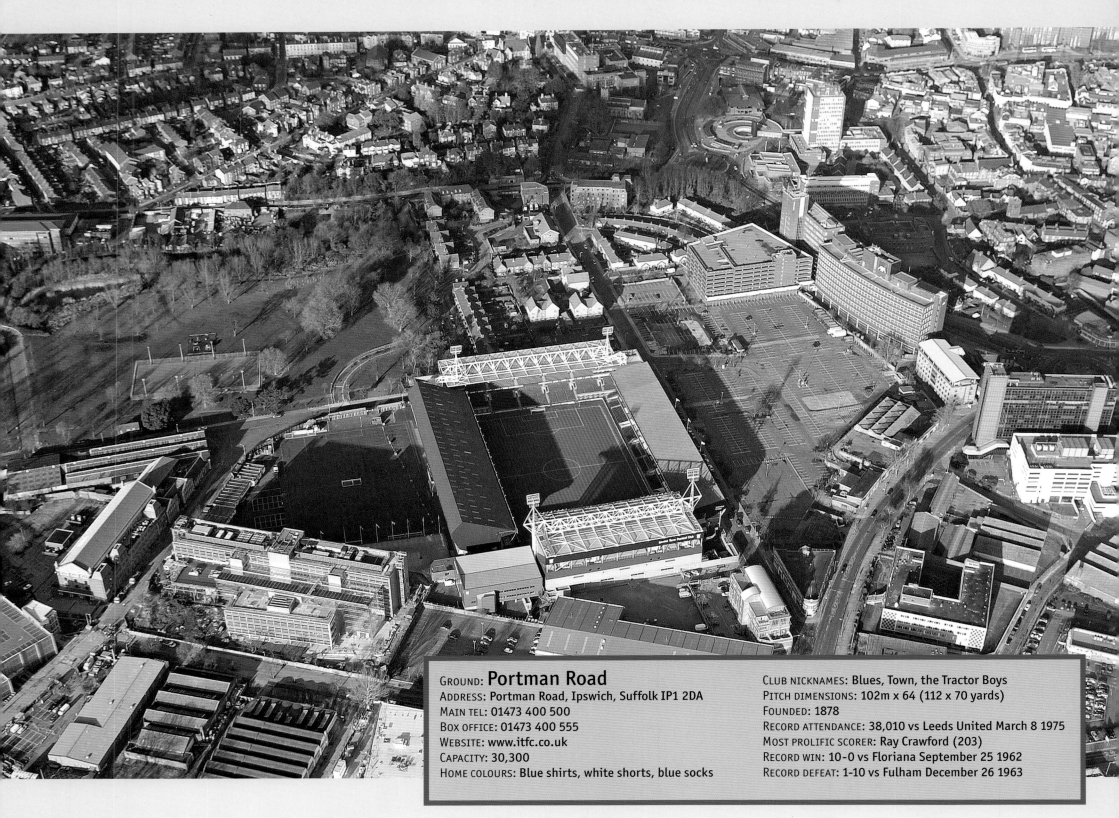

GROUND: **Portman Road**	CLUB NICKNAMES: **Blues, Town, the Tractor Boys**
ADDRESS: **Portman Road, Ipswich, Suffolk IP1 2DA**	PITCH DIMENSIONS: **102m x 64 (112 x 70 yards)**
MAIN TEL: **01473 400 500**	FOUNDED: **1878**
BOX OFFICE: **01473 400 555**	RECORD ATTENDANCE: **38,010 vs Leeds United March 8 1975**
WEBSITE: **www.itfc.co.uk**	MOST PROLIFIC SCORER: **Ray Crawford (203)**
CAPACITY: **30,300**	RECORD WIN: **10-0 vs Floriana September 25 1962**
HOME COLOURS: **Blue shirts, white shorts, blue socks**	RECORD DEFEAT: **1-10 vs Fulham December 26 1963**

IPSWICH TOWN

Ipswich started out as Ipswich AFC in 1878. Their first ground was on Broom Hill, Norwich Road. In 1888 the football team merged with the local rugby team to become Ipswich Town, and they moved to Portman Road, the town's best sporting venue. The rugby team broke away in 1893, but Town continued to share Portman Road with East Suffolk Cricket Club. In 1905 the Ipswich Cricket, Football and Athletic Ground Company formed to pay for separate football and cricket pitches. There was a wooden stand along the Portman Road side, but nothing else divided the two pitches. Portman Road suffered when the army took over the ground during WWI. They refused to leave the ground until 1920, by which time the pitch was ruined. Town eventually turned professional in 1936, but the ground still only had one stand. That summer the club put up fencing and terracing, raising the capacity to 15,000. The following year more terracing was added to the Churchman's End and the club added more seats to the East Stand, both of which were further expanded the next season when Ipswich joined the League in 1939. After WWII the supporters club raised virtually all the money needed to fund improvements until 1965. In 1957 under the management of Alf Ramsay, Ipswich was promoted to Division Two and the club built the West Stand, a two-tier stand with a pitched roof. Between 1972-82 Ipswich continued their footballing successes under Bobby Robson, and the club carried out extensive redevelopments, replacing the East Stand with the Portman Stand. The next major changes took place in the 1980s when the West Stand was extended and renamed the Pioneer Stand. This stand had to be developed just eight years later following the Taylor report when seats were added. Next, seats were installed on both terraces, and in fact Portman Road was the first Premier League ground to become all-seater. The developments continued and the Greene King, or South Stand, opened in 2001, and a year later a new North Stand was opened, bringing the capacity up 30,326.

LEEDS UNITED

Elland Road began its life as an open grass field, known as the Old Peacock ground after the pub opposite. Leeds City Football Club formed in 1904 and took over the ownership of the ground from Holbeck Rugby Club. The West Stand was the first Leeds City built in 1905 and that year more than 22,000 fans saw Leeds City play local rivals Bradford City. During the First World War the army used Elland Road for drilling and shooting practice. Leeds United formed in 1920 from the remnants of Leeds City, which was disbanded after the club was accused of making illegal payments to players. During the 1920s the development of the ground continued with the erection of the so-called Scratching Shed and the Spion Kop. The most impressive transformations came during the late 1960s, however, in the Don Revie era, when support reached record levels. In March 1967 Elland Road saw its highest ever crowd of 57,892 as United battled with Sunderland in the FA Cup. The money the team brought in funded the building of the new Kop in 1968, the season Leeds first became First Division champions, and the Scratching Shed was replaced by the South Sand in 1974. Leeds' performances began to falter and Revie blamed the ground; in 1971 he brought in a gypsy to lift the curse. Revie's theory apparently worked and Leeds won the FA

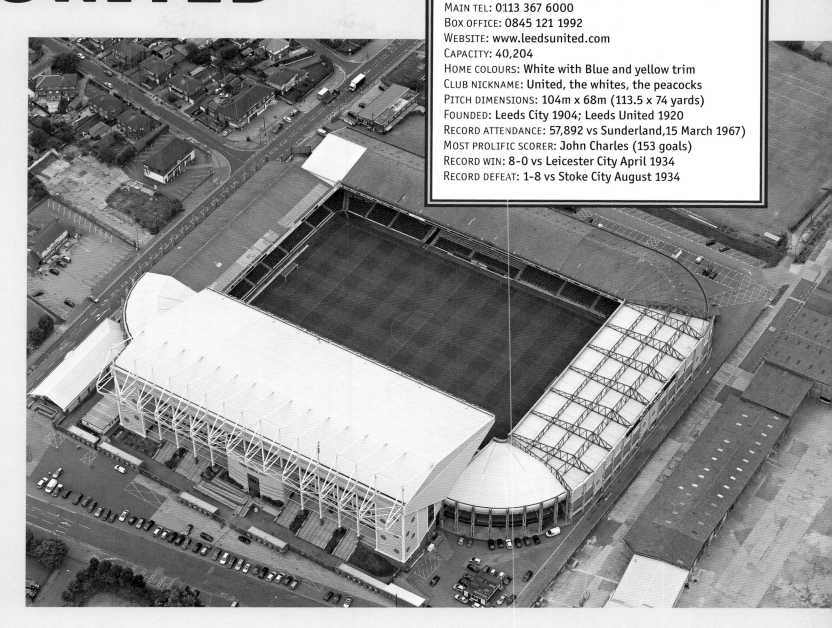

GROUND: **Elland Road**
ADDRESS: Elland Road, Leeds LS11 0ES
MAIN TEL: 0113 367 6000
BOX OFFICE: 0845 121 1992
WEBSITE: www.leedsunited.com
CAPACITY: 40,204
HOME COLOURS: **White with Blue and yellow trim**
CLUB NICKNAME: **United, the whites, the peacocks**
PITCH DIMENSIONS: **104m x 68m (113.5 x 74 yards)**
FOUNDED: **Leeds City 1904; Leeds United 1920**
RECORD ATTENDANCE: **57,892 vs Sunderland,15 March 1967)**
MOST PROLIFIC SCORER: **John Charles (153 goals)**
RECORD WIN: **8-0 vs Leicester City April 1934**
RECORD DEFEAT: **1-8 vs Stoke City August 1934**

Cup the following year (1972) and became Division One champions in 1973-4. Hooliganism blighted the club in the '70s and '80s, and Elland Road became the first club in the country to instal a police compound to hold troublemakers. The East Stand was the last to be completed in 1992-3, the year after Leeds once again won the First Division championship. Now Elland Road boasts the biggest cantilever stand in the world.

LEICESTER CITY

GROUND: **Walkers Stadium**
ADDRESS: Filbert Way, Leicester LE2 7FL
MAIN TEL: 0870 040 6000
BOX OFFICE: 0116 229 4400
WEBSITE: www.lcfc.com
CAPACITY: 32,5000
HOME COLOURS: **Blue shirts, white shorts blue socks**
CLUB NICKNAME: **The Foxes, the Filberts**
PITCH DIMENSIONS: **101m x 66m (110 x 72 yards)**
FOUNDED: **1884**
RECORD ATTENDANCE: **47,298 vs Tottenham Hotspur February 18 1928**
MOST PROLIFIC SCORER: **Arthur Chandler (259)**
RECORD WIN: **10-0 vs Portsmouth October 10 1928**
RECORD DEFEAT: **0-12 vs Nottingham Forest April 21 1909**

Leicester City started out in 1884 as Leicester Fosse as many of the team's founder members lived near Fosse Way in the city's west end. In their first year they played at the racecourse, before moving the following year to Victoria Park. In 1889, Leicester turned professional and moved to Mill Lane, which they left two years later when they found Filbert Street. While the Filbert Street site was being prepared for football, the team played home games at Aylestone Road Cricket Ground. Filbert Street was known then as Walnut Street and the facilities included a low Main Stand. It wasn't until after WWI that Leicester began their major development of the ground and changed their name to Leicester City. In 1921 a new Main Stand was opened, coming complete with a mock classical podium with a small window either side of the players' tunnel and brass rails: a very grand entrance for the players. In 1927 the club built a two-tier stand at the Kop end, and moved the Kop to the Filbert Street End. In February 1928, 47,298 fans crammed in to see the Foxes take on Spurs in the FA Cup, the largest crowd ever at Filbert Street. In the late 1930s the last remaining open section was covered. The next phase of major development was in the 1970s, when the club began converting terraces to seating. The developments started in 1971 with the Filbert Street terrace, which became the North Stand; next the Popular Side was turned into the all-seater East Stand. The 1990s saw further plans for change, and the club considered either building a completely new stand, or turning the pitch 90°. In the end they opted to do neither and rebuilt the Main Stand. However, this was not enough and in 2002 they moved to the all-seater Walkers Stadium. At a cost of £35m, the new stadium is completely enclosed, with all sides the same height and style.

LIVERPOOL

Anfield, Liverpool's ground, was originally home to Everton, who played there from 1884 until 1892, when they fell out with Anfield's owner and moved on to Goodison Park. Anfield's owner, John Houlding, set up his own team, Liverpool, which was dominated by Scots. Major changes took place at Anfield in 1906, the season Liverpool won their second league title. The pitch was raised by five feet and in addition to the two existing covered sides, a new main stand and south terrace were built. The south terrace, the Kop, was one of the tallest terraces in England, complete with 50ft flagpole. The Kop was covered in 1928, when it became Britain's largest covered terrace, with a capacity of 28,000. It was in the era of Liverpool's legendary manager, Bill Shankley in the 1960s that Liverpool carried out further renovations to the ground. The Kemlyn Road Stand was rebuilt and reopened in 1964, the same season that Liverpool won their first FA Cup Final. The 1970s saw the Main Stand extended, and the club began buying houses along Kemlyn Road so they could build a second tier on the Kemlyn Road stand. It wasn't until 1990 when the final residents – two elderly sisters – agreed to sell up.

April 15, 1989 is a day that will forever remain in the memories of Liverpool fans, the date of the Hillsborough disaster, when 96 Liverpool fans were crushed to death. The resulting Taylor report had a massive impact on terraces across the country. Anfield was no different and plans were drawn up to make the Kop all-seater, so that a tragedy on the scale of Hillsborough could not happen again. It was a sad day for many fans in 1994 when the Kop was finally demolished. Liverpool have now announced plans to move to nearby Stanley Park, to a purpose-built 60,000 all-seater stadium, due to open in 2009. The strong ties many fans feel to Anfield means this move is highly unpopular with some.

GROUND: **Anfield**
ADDRESS: **Anfield Road**
MAIN TEL: **0151 263 2361**
BOX OFFICE: **0870 220 2345**
WEBSITE: **www.liverpoolfc.tv**
CAPACITY: **45,362**
HOME COLOURS: **Red shirts, red shorts, red socks**
CLUB NICKNAME: **Reds, Pool**
PITCH DIMENSIONS: **110m x 64m (111 x 74 yards)**
FOUNDED: **1892**
RECORD ATTENDANCE: **61,905 vs Wolverhampton Wanderers February 2 1952**
MOST PROLIFIC SCORER: **Roger Hunt (245)**
RECORD WIN: **10-1 vs Rotherham Town February 18 1896**
RECORD DEFEAT: **1-9 vs Birmingham City December 11 1954**

MANCHESTER CITY

GROUND: **City of Manchester Stadium**
ADDRESS: **City of Manchester Stadium, Sportcity, Rowsley Street, Manchester M11 3FF**
MAIN TEL: **0161 231 3200**
BOX OFFICE: **0870 062 1894**
WEBSITE: **www.mcfc.co.uk**
CAPACITY: **48,000**
HOME COLOURS: **Laser blue shirts, white shorts, navy socks**
CLUB NICKNAME: **The Blues, the Citizens**
PITCH DIMENSIONS: **107m x 71m (117 x 78 yards)**
FOUNDED: **1887**
RECORD ATTENDANCE: **84,569 vs Stoke City March 3 1934**
MOST PROLIFIC SCORER: **Tommy Johnson (158)**
RECORD WIN: **10-1 vs Huddersfield November 7 1987**
RECORD DEFEAT: **1-9 vs Everton September 3 1906**

Manchester City's roots date back to an amalgamation between local teams West Gorton and Gorton Athletic in 1887. At first they played as Ardwick, before changing their name to Manchester City in 1894. They played games on Hyde Road, a small ground penned in by a railway line and houses, but it had two stands, paid for with the help of a local brewery. When, in 1920, the Main Stand burned down, the club decided it was time to move. At the start of the 1923 season the club opened the doors to their new ground, Maine Road. The ground was vast; in the 1920s it had a capacity in excess of 80,000 and regular gates of 37,000, the highest gates in the League. In 1934, 84,569 fans turned out to see City take on Stoke in the Cup. Following WWII local rivals Manchester United became lodgers at Maine Road, and profits soared. They spent some of this money on wooden benches, which were installed under the Platt Lane roof in the 1950s. In 1956 City won their third FA Cup and built a roof over the Kippax terrace, leaving just the Scoreboard End uncovered. This end was replaced by the North Stand in 1971. In 1983 the club replaced the roof on the Main Stand. Following the Taylor report, in 1992 the Platt Lane Stand was demolished and replaced by the Umbro Stand, which cost City £5m and plunged the club into debt. The report's requirements meant the club had to demolish the Kippax terrace and replace it with an all-seater stand. The new stand cost £11m, and brought Maine Road's capacity up to 32,344. Despite spending £19m on developments, in 2003 the club left Maine Road and became tenants of the brand new City of Manchester Stadium, built for the 2002 Commonwealth Games. The club spent £20m turning the athletics stadium into a football ground, expanding the stands and bringing them closer to the pitch. The bowl-shaped stadium has a capacity of 48,000 and is totally enclosed with two three-tiered stands and two two-tiered stands.

MANCHESTER UNITED

Manchester United started out as Newton Heath FC, formed by railway workers from the Lancashire and Yorkshire Railway in 1878. The Heathens played early matches on North Road, before moving to Bank Street, Clayton in 1893, a year after joining the League. By 1902 their debts had grown so large they went into liquidation. Local brewer John H Davies rescued the club and changed their name to Manchester United. Their fortunes also changed; by 1906 they were back in the First Division and had cover on all sides of the ground, a Main Stand with a gallery and a total capacity of 50,000. In 1908, United won their first League title, and the FA Cup in 1909. A year later the club said farewell to Bank Street and moved five miles away to a new ground, Old Trafford. By then Davies had invested £60,000 developing the ground, a rectangle with curved corners and a multi-span Main Stand. In 1931 United were relegated, crowds dropped to 3,500 and United faced bankruptcy for the second time. Up stepped James Gibson, a wealthy businessman, who cleared the club's debts and funded a cover over the United Road side. The ground was badly damaged during the Second World War and United began ground sharing with Manchester City. It wasn't until 1949 that Old Trafford was repaired and United returned. The pitched roof covering the south-west corner was expanded to cover the Stretford End in 1959, the year after the Munich air crash. The 1960s saw further developments at the ground, when Old Trafford was selected as a venue for World Cup games. In 1965 they built a new two-tier stand over the United Road terrace capable of seating 10,000 and holding a further 10,000 standing. This new stand also held the first executive boxes at a European football ground. From then until the 1990s United gradually converted Old Trafford into a fully enclosed all-seater stadium. New plans to expand capacity were drawn up in 1995 and a three-tiered North Stand opened in 1996 and second tiers were added to the East and West Stands in 2001. In 2006 North-East and North-West quadrants were opened bringing the capacity to 76,212.

GROUND: **Old Trafford**
ADDRESS: **Old Trafford, Sir Matt Busby Way, Manchester M16 0RA**
MAIN TEL: **0870 442 1994**
BOX OFFICE: **0870 442 1999**
WEBSITE: **www.manutd.com**
CAPACITY: **76,212**
HOME COLOURS: **Red shirts, white shorts, black socks**
CLUB NICKNAME: **Red Devils**
PITCH DIMENSIONS: **105m x 69m (115 x 76 yards)**
FOUNDED: **1878**
RECORD ATTENDANCE: **76,078 vs Aston Villa, January 13 2007**
MOST PROLIFIC SCORER: **Bobby Charlton (199)**
RECORD WIN: **10-0 vs Anderlecht September 26 1956**
RECORD DEFEAT: **0-7 vs Blackburn Rovers April 10 1926**

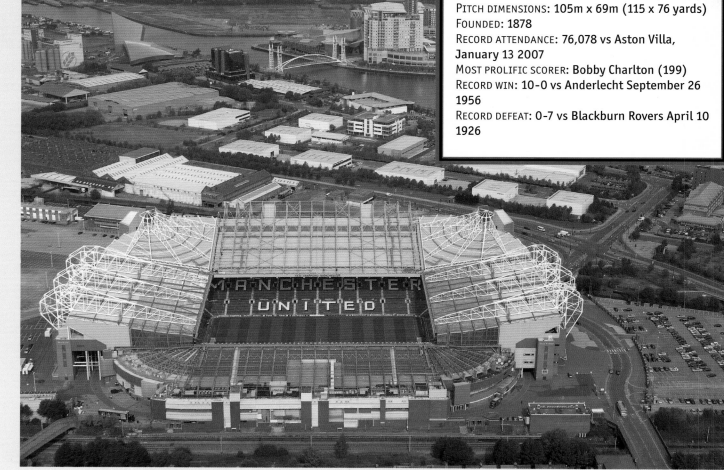

MIDDLESBROUGH

Middlesbrough formed in 1876, although they didn't find themselves a proper home until 1879, when they moved to Breckon Hill Road, and again a year later to Middlesbrough Cricket Club, Linthorpe Road. At Linthorpe Road the club built a small stand, and in 1899 Boro joined the League. By 1902 it was clear the ground was too small, and in 1903 they moved to Ayresome Park. Scottish architect Archibald Leitch helped the club in their mission to prepare the ground and build a stadium in nine months. He built a two-tier stand with a semi-circular gable and barrel roof, capable of seating 2,000, banking at both ends and transported the old stand from Linthorpe Road. The next major developments came in the 1930s when the South Stand was replaced by a two-tier stand and the West End was given a roof. After the War the club made further improvements to the terracing, and in 1949 the ground held a record 53,596 fans as Boro took on Newcastle. Ayresome Park was selected as a venue for some of the 1966 World Cup matches, and the club, undertook a number of major ground improvements, including adding a roof to the East End and seats to the North, South and East terraces. In the following years Middlesbrough's success faltered and support dwindled. In 1986, fire safety checks revealed the ground needed significant attention, and owing to Middlesbrough's huge debts, they were locked out of Ayresome Park and forced to play home games at Hartlepool. The ground had £800,000 spent on it following the Taylor report, fences were removed, seats installed in the South and East Stands and plans laid out for redeveloping the North Stand. However, in 1994 self-made millionaire Steve Gibson took over a 68 per cent share in the club and in April 1995 the club played their last game at Ayresome Park. At a cost of £12m, the club have now moved to the site of a former petro-chemical storage facility. The stadium is now totally enclosed with a two-tiered West Stand and single tiers on the other three sides. The capacity is now 35,100.

GROUND: **Cellnet Riverside Stadium**
ADDRESS: **Riverside Stadium, Middlesbrough, Cleveland TS3 6RS**
MAIN TEL: **01642 877700**
BOX OFFICE: **01642 877745**
WEBSITE: **www.mfc.co.uk**
CAPACITY: **35,100**
HOME COLOURS: **Red shirts with white trim, red shorts, red socks**
CLUB NICKNAME: **Boro**
PITCH DIMENSIONS: **105m x 69m (115 x 75 yards)**
FOUNDED: **1876**
RECORD ATTENDANCE: **53,596 vs Newcastle United December 27 1949**
MOST PROLIFIC SCORER: **George Camsell (326)**
RECORD WIN: **9-0 vs Brighton and Hove Albion August 23 1958**
RECORD DEFEAT: **0-9 vs Blackburn Rovers November 6 1954**

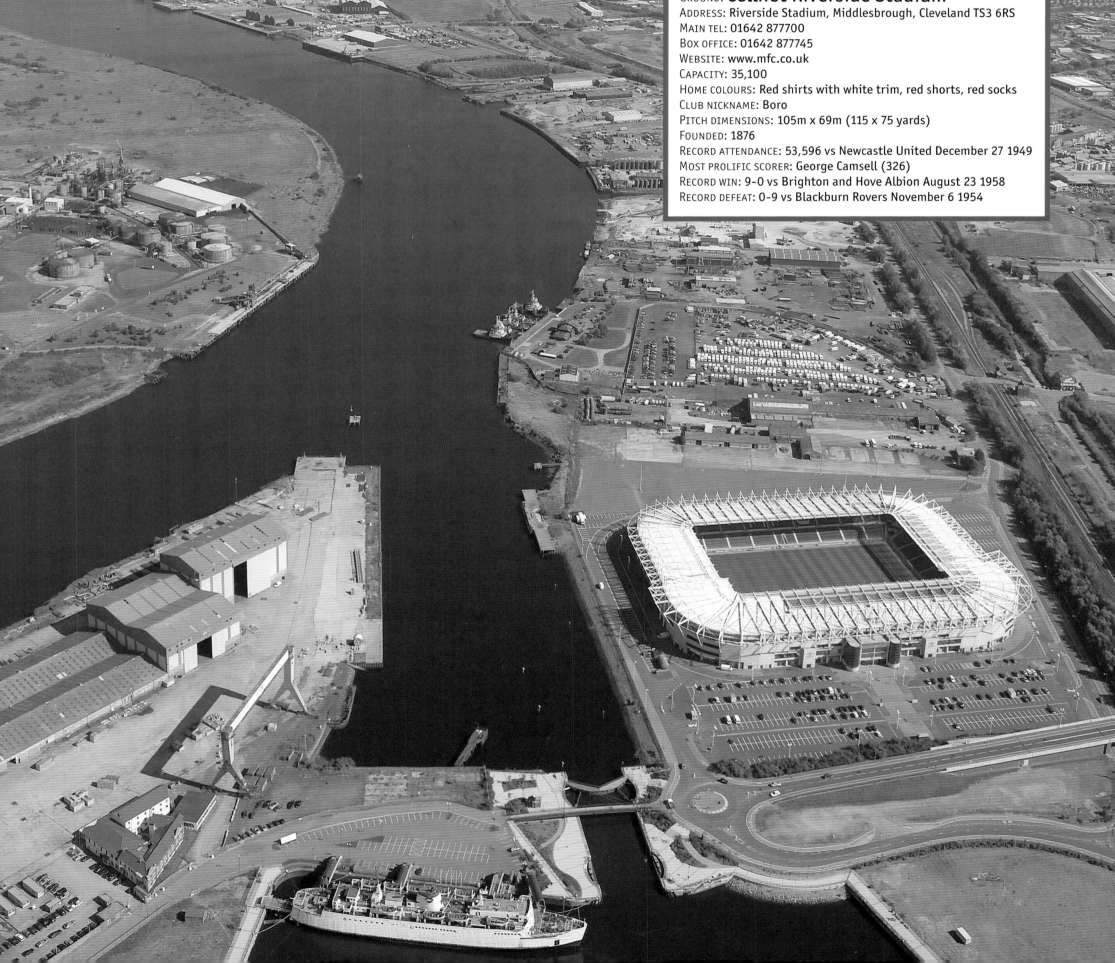

MILLENNIUM STADIUM

The Millennium Stadium was opened in October 1999 on the site of Cardiff Arms Park. The ground dates back to the 17th century, but was first called Cardiff Arms Park in 1787. Cricket was the first sport played at the ground from 1848; rugby was played there from 1876. A Grandstand was opened in 1885, a year before football was first played there. An extension to the Grandstand was added in 1890, and a grand pavilion was built in 1904. The Grandstand was replaced by a South Stand in 1912. The Park's owner, Lord Bute, sold the ground in 1922 and the rugby and cricket company set up a joint company to take over the ground. A North Stand opened in 1934 and a South Stand was built in 1956 after Cardiff was selected to stage the 1958 Commonwealth Games. In 1968, the North Stand was demolished as the Welsh Rugby Union took over Cardiff Arms Park and there followed a 16-year period of redevelopment. A new two-tiered stand was erected in place of the North Stand. The East Terrace opened in 1980, and finally a South Stand opened in 1984. Football returned to Cardiff Arms Park in 1989. Just six years later the WRU decided that the ground's 53,500 capacity was not enough. They submitted plans to the Millennium Commission for an ambitious 75,000-seater stadium to be created on the site of the park. The Commission stumped up £50 million and the other £114

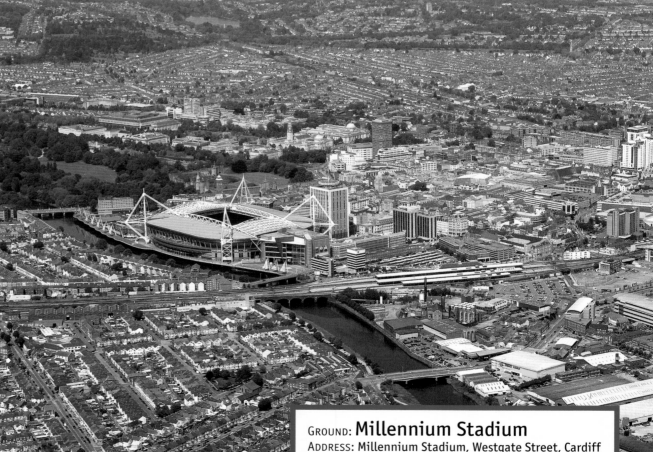

million was funded by commercial sources. The ground was built in time for the 1999 Rugby World Cup and quickly established itself as a unique sporting venue. The Millennium Stadium has Britain's only retractable roof, and the pitch is grown outside the ground and brought in when needed. It is completely enclosed with curved corners and three tiers on three sides, with the north stand remaining a two-tier structure as it backs on to a rugby club, leaving no room for a third tier. The ground's capacity is now 74,500. The ground now stages FA Cup Finals, play-off finals, British Speedway Grand Prix and pop concerts.

GROUND: **Millennium Stadium**
ADDRESS: Millennium Stadium, Westgate Street, Cardiff **CF10 1JA**
MAIN TEL: 0870 013 8600
BOX OFFICE: 029 2023 1458
WEBSITE: www.millenniumstadium.com
CAPACITY: 74,500
PITCH DIMENSIONS: 101m x 66m (110 yards x 72 yards)
OPENED: 1999
PREVIOUS NAME: **Cardiff Arms Park**

MILLWALL

Millwall Rovers was formed in 1885 by workers from Morton's Jam factory on the Isle of Dogs. Most of the workers at the factory were Scottish, so the kit was blue and white to reflect the Scottish flag. The club played at four different grounds on the Isle of Dogs and changed their name to Millwall Athletic, before finally relocating south of the river to the Den, Cold Blow Lane, in 1910. When the Den opened, only the main stand had been built, with banking on the other three sides. In 1920 Millwall joined league division three and dropped Athletic from its name. The ground developed during the following decade, and saw its highest attendance of 48,672 in an FA Cup tie against Derby County on February 20, 1937. The Second World War came just when Millwall were forming a strong side. Docklands suffered badly during the Blitz and the Main Stand was severely damaged. With compensation from the War Damages Commission, the club began rebuilding the stands. They covered the Ilderton Road end in 1947 and the two remaining sides during the 1950s. Little changed inside the ground for the next 40 years, except an extension to the Ilderton Road end and seating in the paddock. Millwall played their last game at the Den in 1993, 83 years after arriving. They moved a quarter of a mile away to the New Den, a 20,000 all-seater stadium at a cost of £16m. There were many reasons for this move, not least the hope that livelier elements of some sections of the Millwall faithful might be tamed by the constrictions of an all-seater stadium. Similar to the old Den, the new ground was designed by Scottish architects and engineers. The New Den consists of four stands which, from inside the stadium, appear almost identical. In fact only the North and South Stands are identical.

GROUND: **The New Den**
ADDRESS: **Zampa Road, Bermondsey, London SE16 3LN**
MAIN TEL: **020 7232 1222**
BOX OFFICE: **020 7413 3357**
WEBSITE: **www.millwallfc.co.uk**
CAPACITY: **20,146**
HOME COLOURS: **Blue shirt, white shorts, blue socks**
CLUB NICKNAME: **The Lions**
PITCH DIMENSIONS: **102m x 68m (112 x 74 yards)**
FOUNDED: **1885**
RECORD ATTENDANCE: **48,672 vs Derby County February 1937**
MOST PROLIFIC SCORER: **Teddy Sheringham (93)**
RECORD WIN: **9-1 vs Torquay United September 29 1927**
RECORD DEFEAT: **1-9 vs Aston Villa January 28 1946**

NEWCASTLE UNITED

Newcastle United began life as East End FC. They formed in 1881 and used to play at Chillingham Road in Heaton; they moved to St James' Park in 1892. The facilities were very basic and the pitch had a distinctive slant. Following their promotion in 1898, the ground's capacity of 15,000 was severely stretched. The next year an extra four acres were leased to the club, so they moved the pitch and tons of soil to reduce the pitch's slant. They cut terracing into the banks of the Leazes Park End and Leazes Terrace. In 1905, after losing the Cup Final but winning the League, Newcastle drew the largest crowds in the League, so they began revamping the stadium. The wooden stands were cleared, three sides of banking were expanded, terraced and wire barriers added. A West Stand was built with seating for 4,680; beneath this stand was a swimming pool for the players.

The ground opened in November 1905 with its new capacity of 65,000. The 1920s saw more improvements, with yet another pitch laid. A new cover was put on the Leazes Park End in 1930, and plans were drawn up to extend the other sides, although the council rejected these. The same year, 68,386 fans saw Newcastle take on Chelsea, a record attendance; during this time the average gate was over 56,000. The Magpies had three FA Cup victories between 1951-55, which sent profits soaring, however every attempt to expand the ground was rejected, and a feud developed between the club and the council. In 1971 the club were finally granted a 99-year lease on the ground and permission to build a new 3,400 seat stand backing on to Leazes Terrace. The next major development came in 1987 when the 6,607 seat Jackie Milburn Stand was built. Sir John Hall joined the board in 1992, and he took full control of the club in 1994. He spent £23.5m on completely redeveloping St James' Park, with all-seater stands at each end and corner, and additional tiers on the north and west sides, and the north-west corner, raising capacity to 52,218.

GROUND: **St James' Park**
ADDRESS: **St James' Park, Newcastle-Upon-Tyne NE1 4ST**
MAIN TEL: **0191 201 8400**
BOX OFFICE: **0191 261 1571**
WEBSITE: **www.nufc.co.uk**
CAPACITY: **52,218**
HOME COLOURS: **Black and white striped shirts with blue trim, black shorts, black socks with white trim**
CLUB NICKNAMES: **The Magpies, the Toon**
PITCH DIMENSIONS: **101m x 67m (110 x 73 yards)**
FOUNDED: **1881**
RECORD ATTENDANCE: **68,386 vs Chelsea September 3 1930**
MOST PROLIFIC SCORER: **Alan Shearer 206**
RECORD WIN: **13-0 vs Newport County October 5 1946**
RECORD DEFEAT: **0-9 vs Burton Wanderers April 15 1895**

NORWICH CITY

Football has been played in Norwich since 1868, but Norwich City did not form until 1902. The ground the team initially used belonged to Norwich County FA on Newmarket Road. The Canaries turned professional in 1905, yet there were problems with their rented ground. Their chairman, John Pyke, thought he had solved these when he bought a disused chalk pit on Rosary Road. A wooden stand was brought with the club to the new ground, which labourers spent the summer of 1908 preparing for football. The ground was named the Nest, but it was not a particularly suitable home for the Canaries, with houses very close to the pitch at the west end and a steep concrete verge at the east end. In 1922 barriers on top of the verge collapsed and a boy was badly injured. Despite the problems, the club continued to play on the ground until 1935. That year, the club moved to Carrow Road, a sports ground owned by Colman's Mustard. In just 82 days the club built a 3,500-seater main stand and paddock on one side and embankments on the other three sides. In 1937 the first terrace cover went up at the Station End, renamed the

Barclay End, but it wasn't until 1959, when the Canaries reached the semi-finals of the FA Cup and won promotion, that they could afford further ground improvements. The terrace opposite the Main Stand was covered and in 1963 the South Stand was built. Fire destroyed the central section of the Main Stand in October 1984, which was replaced the following season. The 1990s saw the ground almost completely rebuilt, with new stands on each side. The most recent to be opened is the Jarrold Road South Stand in 2004; this can hold 8,000 fans. There are two-tiered stands at either end and the Geoffrey Watling City Stand is a smaller single-tiered stand. The total capacity is now 24,700.

GROUND: **Carrow Road**

ADDRESS: **Carrow Road, Norwich NR1 1JE**
MAIN TEL: **01603 760 760**
BOX OFFICE: **0870 444 1902**
WEBSITE: **www.canaries.co.uk**
CAPACITY: **24,700**
HOME COLOURS: **Yellow shirts, green shorts**
CLUB NICKNAME: **The Canaries**
PITCH DIMENSIONS: **101m x 69m (114 x 75 yards)**
FOUNDED: **1902**
RECORD ATTENDANCE: **43,984 vs Leicester City March 3 1963**
MOST PROLIFIC SCORER: **Johnny Gavin (122)**
RECORD WIN: **10-2 vs Coventry City March 15 1930**
RECORD DEFEAT: **2-10 vs Swindon Town September 5 1908**

NOTTINGHAM FOREST

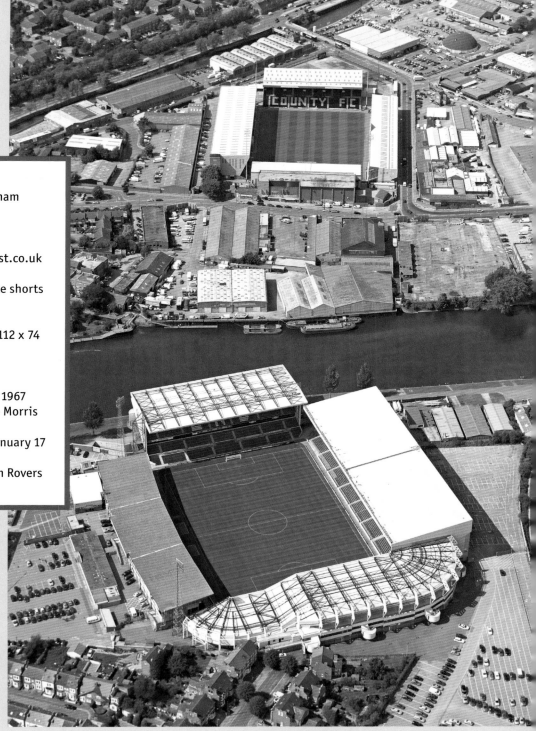

Nottingham Forest formed in 1865, and played their first games at the Forest Recreation Ground. They moved in 1879 to the Meadows, and just a year later moved again to Trent Bridge, the cricket ground. The club then had a number of different homes and it wasn't until 1890 that Forest settled for a while at the Town Ground. It cost the club £1,000 to prepare the ground for football. Forest joined the League in 1892 and in 1898 they won their first FA Cup Final. Their success brought increased numbers of supporters and that year they moved to the City ground. It cost £3,000 to prepare the ground. The club built a wooden Main Stand and a wooden shelter at the Trent End. The City Ground survived the War with very little damage – it cost more to repair the ground when the Trent burst its banks in 1947. After winning the Third Division title in 1950 the club drew up plans to redevelop the ground. In 1954 the Trent End terrace was extended and covered, and three years later the club built an East Stand and expanded the Bridgford End terrace. Between 1962-65 the club redeveloped the Main Stand, in time for Forest's highest gate ever when 49,946 fans saw them take on Manchester United in 1967. The following season fire engulfed the Main Stand in a game against Leeds United – fortunately no fans were injured. The club had to move temporarily to Meadow Lane, Notts County's ground, for six games while the City Ground was repaired. The late 1970s saw Forest win the League title, the European Cup and the League Cup twice in successive seasons. The money earned from this success funded the building of the two-tiered, all-seater Executive Stand (now called the Brian Clough Stand) in place of the East Stand, costing a cool £2.5m. After a wrangle with the council over a strip of land behind the Trent End, Forest began developing the Bridgford End in 1992, followed shortly afterwards by the Trent End which brought capacity to 30,000.

GROUND: **City Ground**
ADDRESS: City Ground, Nottingham NG2 5FJ
MAIN TEL: 0115 982 4444
BOX OFFICE: 0115 982 4445
WEBSITE: www.nottinghamforest.co.uk
CAPACITY: 30,602
HOME COLOURS: Red shirts, white shorts with red trim, red socks
CLUB NICKNAME: The Reds
PITCH DIMENSIONS: 102m x 68 (112 x 74 yards)
FOUNDED: 1865
RECORD ATTENDANCE: 49,946 vs Manchester United October 28 1967
MOST PROLIFIC SCORER: Grenville Morris (119)
RECORD WIN: 14-0 vs Clapton January 17 1891
RECORD DEFEAT: 1-9 vs Blackburn Rovers April 10 1937

PORTSMOUTH

Portsmouth formed in 1898 after the town's other football club, the Royal Artillery, were suspended by the FA for breaching amateur regulations. The club bought land near Fratton railway station. Fratton Park was opened in September 1899. The club progressed well at the start of the 20th century, generating enough money to build a mock-Tudor pavilion at the Frogmore Road entrance, complete with clock tower. In 1920 the club joined the League and were soon promoted to division two. In 1925 they opened the South Stand, which had 4,000 seats, a paddock and a balcony. Despite losing in the Cup Finals in 1929 and 1934, their profits continued to rise and they were able to fund the building of the north stand in 1935. Pompey finally got their hands on the FA Cup in 1939, when they thrashed Wolves 4-1. After WWII, Portsmouth won the League in 1949 and 1950, and were drawing average gates of 39,000. They notched up their largest crowd ever in February 1949 when 51,385 people saw them take on Derby County in the FA Cup. The Fratton End was covered in 1956, but it wasn't until 1988 that any further developments took place at Fratton Park. Jim Gregory bought the club and between 1988-94 funded a £4m refurbishment programme. The Fratton End was demolished in 1988, but plans for the replacement all-seater stand had to be shelved when British Rail refused to sell any land behind the ground. In April 1993 the club unveiled plans for a move to Parkway Stadium in Farlington, although these were turned down by Whitehall. In 1995 the ground was partly rebuilt and made all-seater bringing the capacity up to 19,214. Following the club's successful promotion to the Premiership in 2003, there are plans to massively redevelop the ground. The pitch will be rotated 90°, and the stands developed to bring the capacity up to 28,000. It is hoped the new Fratton Park will open at the start of the 2005-6 season, at a cost of £26m.

GROUND: **Fratton Park**
ADDRESS: Fratton Park, Frogmore Road, Portsmouth PO4 8RA
MAIN TEL: 023 9273 1204
BOX OFFICE: 0871 230 1898
WEBSITE: www.pompeyfc.co.uk
CAPACITY: 19,214
HOME COLOURS: Blue shirts, white shorts, red socks
CLUB NICKNAME: Pompey
PITCH DIMENSIONS: 101m x 66m (110 x 72 yards)
FOUNDED: 1898
RECORD ATTENDANCE: 51,385 vs Derby County February 26 1949
MOST PROLIFIC SCORER: Peter Harris (194)
RECORD WIN: 9-1 vs Notts County April 9 1927
RECORD DEFEAT: 0-10 vs Leicester City October 20 1928

RANGERS

Rangers was formed in 1873 and the club played its first games on Glasgow Green. They moved twice before arriving at Ibrox in 1887, to a ground which borders their current ground. The original Ibrox was a success and hosted the 1890 Cup Final and three internationals; however when local rivals Celtic opened the more sophisticated Celtic Park, Rangers began looking for a grander ground. In 1899, after winning the League without losing a game, Rangers began building on the land next door. When it opened it boasted an oval track, a pavilion and a stand. In 1900 Scottish architect Archibald Leitch built terracing behind the west goal, capable of holding 36,000 fans. However, the terracing was shaky and in a game between England and Scotland in 1902 this collapsed, killing 26 and injuring 500. By 1910 Leitch had been consulted on expanding Ibrox to increase its capacity to 63,000.

GROUND: Ibrox Stadium
ADDRESS: Ibrox Stadium Glasgow, G51 2XD
MAIN TEL: 0141 427 8500
BOX OFFICE: 0870 600 1993
WEBSITE: www.rangers.co.uk
CAPACITY: 50,403
HOME COLOURS: Blue, red and white
CLUB NICKNAME: The Gers
PITCH DIMENSIONS: 105m x 69m (115 x 75 yards)
FOUNDED: 1873
RECORD ATTENDANCE: 118,567 vs Celtic January 2 1939
MOST PROLIFIC SCORER: Ally McCoist (355)
RECORD WIN: 13-0 vs Possilpark October 6 1877
RECORD DEFEAT: 1-7 vs Celtic October 19 1957

Rangers won the League and Cup double in 1928 and this funded the building of a 10,000 seat double-decker South Stand. The Gers continued to enlarge the banking and in 1939 a record 118,567 turned up for an Old Firm derby. Tragedy struck again at Ibrox in 1971, when 66 people died and 145 were injured as the notorious Stairway 13 in the ground's north-east corner collapsed at the end of a game against Celtic. Following the tragedy, the club planned to completely rebuild all sides except for Leith's South Stand, and would make the three new stands all-seater. Work began in 1978 and the new Ibrox opened in 1981 at a cost of £10m. However, hard times followed and attendances dropped. Heavy investment in 1986 saw the club's fortunes reverse and in 1988 they spent £4m on the rear of the Govan Stand. Yet more investment came when new chairman, David Murray took over; he spent £20m adding another tier to the South Stand, making it all-seater. An innovative move to increase capacity involved the lowering of the pitch by 12 inches, in 1991, and in 1996 the corners at either side of the Govan stand were filled in, bringing Ibrox's all-seated capacity up to 50,403.

SOUTHAMPTON

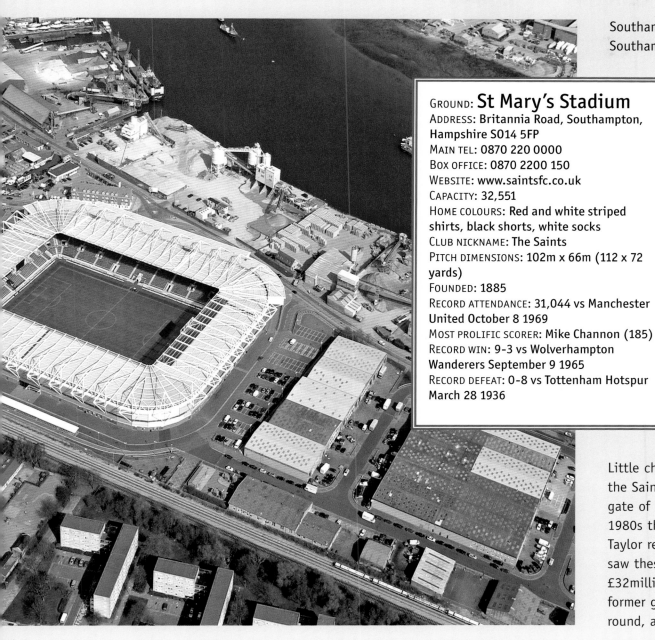

Southampton FC was founded in 1885. They originally called themselves Southampton St Mary's FC, because of their ties with the local St Mary's church. The team played their first games on the site of the County Bowling Club. Just a year later they moved to the Antelope Cricket Ground, which had previously been the home of Hampshire County Cricket Club. The team were relatively successful and turned professional in 1894. Two years later they changed their name to Southampton FC, and in 1898 they moved to the Dell. Fortune shone on the Saints, as a local fish merchant, George Thomas, funded the development of the Dell. Both ends were terraced and stands were erected on the East and West sides. Their fortunes off the pitch were not matched on the pitch, and by 1906 there was talk the club may have to leave the Dell as their debts were soaring. They remained however, and joined the third division in 1920, winning promotion to the second just two years later. This success meant they were able to expand the ground, and they began with an £8,000 extension of the East Stand. In 1927 the West Stand was torn down and a new one was erected in 1928. The late 1940s saw high attendances at the Dell and three concrete platforms were fixed above the Milton Road End terrace, known as the chocolate boxes.

Little changed at the Dell for the following 30 years. During that time the Saints won promotion to the top flight, and attracted their record gate of 31,044 in a league game against Manchester United. By the early 1980s the club had already begun to think of leaving the Dell, as the Taylor report brought the ground's capacity down to 15,352. The 1990s saw these plans become a reality, and in August 2001, the new £32million all-seater St Mary's stadium was opened on the site of a former gasworks. The totally enclosed stadium has one tier all the way round, and has a much healthier capacity of 32,551.

GROUND: **St Mary's Stadium**
ADDRESS: **Britannia Road, Southampton, Hampshire SO14 5FP**
MAIN TEL: 0870 220 0000
BOX OFFICE: 0870 2200 150
WEBSITE: www.saintsfc.co.uk
CAPACITY: 32,551
HOME COLOURS: **Red and white striped shirts, black shorts, white socks**
CLUB NICKNAME: **The Saints**
PITCH DIMENSIONS: **102m x 66m (112 x 72 yards)**
FOUNDED: 1885
RECORD ATTENDANCE: **31,044 vs Manchester United October 8 1969**
MOST PROLIFIC SCORER: **Mike Channon (185)**
RECORD WIN: **9-3 vs Wolverhampton Wanderers September 9 1965**
RECORD DEFEAT: **0-8 vs Tottenham Hotspur March 28 1936**

SUNDERLAND

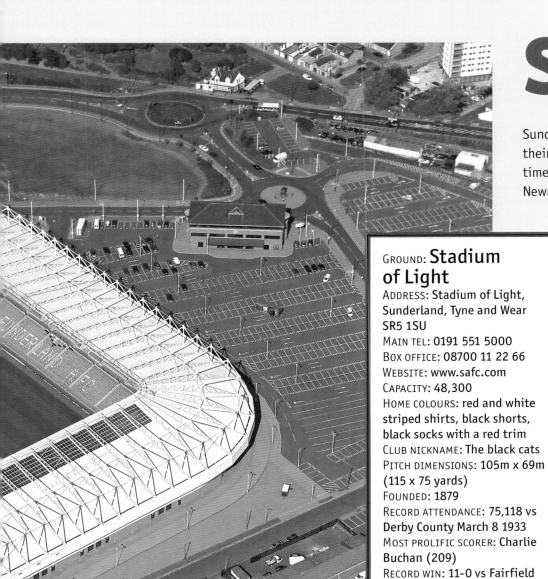

Sunderland AFC was formed in 1879 by Glaswegian teacher Jimmy Allen. They played their first games at Blue House field, close to Allen's school. They moved four more times before settling, albeit temporarily, at the district's then best ground on Newcastle Road. The ground was already enclosed on three sides, so the club only had to build one further stand on the east side. In 1888 a new boss took over at Newcastle Road, who proved very successful. He brought in new players and after joining the League in 1890, they won three successive championships. The team's success meant increasing support, and it was not long before the club had to look for a new ground. In 1898 they moved to Roker Park, where the club would stay for 99 years. During the summer two stands were built – a Grandstand and the Clock Stand, with the other two ends being left open. In 1908 the capacity of Roker Park was 50,000. The 1920s saw further developments; in 1925 the Fulwell End was expanded bringing capacity up to 60,000, and the Main Stand was erected in 1929. March 8, 1933 saw a record 75,811 fans packing into Roker Park to see Sunderland take on Derby County in the FA Cup. The Clock Stand was replaced in 1936, and no further developments took place until after the war. Roker Park was selected as a venue to stage games during the 1966 World Cup, which led to the pitch being expanded by three yards, the addition of seats in the Clock Stand and the Fulwell End was covered. The next major changes came in the 1990s when, following the Taylor report, the club had to decide whether to redevelop or relocate. After a lengthy battle with the nearby Nissan car plant, a new site was found in 1996, on what used to be the Monkwearmouth Colliery. The Stadium of Light opened in 1997, with three two-tier stands on the north, south and east sides linking to the Main Stand on the west. The capacity was expanded to 48,300 in 2001 when the North Stand and north-west corner were expanded to three tiers.

GROUND: **Stadium of Light**
ADDRESS: **Stadium of Light, Sunderland, Tyne and Wear SR5 1SU**
MAIN TEL: 0191 551 5000
BOX OFFICE: 08700 11 22 66
WEBSITE: www.safc.com
CAPACITY: 48,300
HOME COLOURS: **red and white striped shirts, black shorts, black socks with a red trim**
CLUB NICKNAME: **The black cats**
PITCH DIMENSIONS: **105m x 69m (115 x 75 yards)**
FOUNDED: 1879
RECORD ATTENDANCE: **75,118 vs Derby County March 8 1933**
MOST PROLIFIC SCORER: **Charlie Buchan (209)**
RECORD WIN: **11-0 vs Fairfield February 2 1895**
RECORD DEFEAT: **0-8 vs West Ham United October 19 1968**

TOTTENHAM HOTSPUR

Tottenham Hotspur was formed by a group of cricketers in 1882. The team, then called Hotspur FC, first played games on Tottenham Marshes. By 1885, they had added the prefix "Tottenham" and three years later the team moved to their first proper ground, Northumberland Park. In 1899 the club moved to a ground owned by a local brewery then called the High Road Ground. Spurs became the first non-league team since 1888 to win the FA Cup in 1901. The first major stand to be built was the West Stand, opened in 1909. The stand came complete with a mock-Tudor gable and a year later a copper cockerel perched on a ball was placed on the roof. In 1919 the ground adopted the name of the local station – White Hart Lane. Spurs won the FA Cup for the second time in 1921, and this funded the covering of the Paxton Road End and the Park Lane End. It was not until 1934 that the final terrace – the East terrace – was built on. The East Stand was a two-tier stand erected on top of the terracing, so it looked to be three tiers.

This stand had a capacity of 24,000, and when Spurs took Sunderland on in the FA Cup in 1938, a record 75,038 fans looked on. The cockerel moved to the East Stand in 1958, in time to see the club go through their most successful era, winning the double in 1961, the FA Cup in 1962 and '67, the League Cup in 1971 and 1973, the European Cup in 1963 and the UEFA Cup in 1972. The 1980s saw the club nearly bankrupted as the building of the West Stand cost almost double the original fee. The redevelopment of the East Stand in 1987 again caused crippling debt as costs spiralled. However, the club managed its debts and after adding seats to the East terrace, the Park Lane terrace and the Shelf, a new South Stand was built in 1995, and a new upper tier was added to the Paxton Road End, bringing the capacity up to 36,211.

GROUND: **White Hart Lane**
ADDRESS: 748 High Road Tottenham London N17 0AP
MAIN TEL: 020 8365 5000
BOX OFFICE: 0870 420 5000
WEBSITE: www.spurs.co.uk
CAPACITY: 36,211
HOME COLOURS: White shirts, navy blue shorts, navy blue socks
CLUB NICKNAME: Spurs
PITCH DIMENSIONS: 101m x 67m (110 x 73 yards)
FOUNDED: 1882
RECORD ATTENDANCE: 75,038 vs Sunderland March 5 1938
MOST PROLIFIC SCORER: Jimmy Greaves (220)
RECORD WIN: 13-2 vs Crewe Alexandra February 3 1960
RECORD DEFEAT: 0-7 vs Liverpool September 2 1978

WEMBLEY

Sports were played on the site occupied by Wembley stadium as far back as the 1880s when Wembley Park Leisure Grounds had football and cricket pitches and a running track. In 1889 the owners decided to build a main attraction at the site, and began work on a huge four-legged tower. Work began, but was never completed and in 1907 what had been built was dynamited. The first Wembley Stadium was dreamt up by the government in 1918 following WWI. Plans were laid for a British Empire Exhibition, with a national sporting stadium as the centrepiece. Originally named the Empire Stadium, architects John Simpson and Maxwell Ayerton built Wembley; it took just 300 days to complete. George V officially opened the Empire Exhibition in 1924, although the first event held there was the White Horse Cup Final in 1923 between West Ham United and Bolton Wanderers. During that game the stadium's official capacity of 126,047 was far exceeded and an estimated 200,000 people crammed in to see the game. The ground was oval-shaped and the pitch was surrounded by a running track. The north and south ends of the stadium had seated stands, while the remaining sides had open terracing. Floodlights were added to the stadium in 1955, and the encircling roof and electronic scoreboards were added in 1963. In 1990, following the Taylor report, the ground became all-seater and had a capacity of 80,000. Apart from this, very little changed in the stadium's structure from its original 1920s design. The stadium has been used for a wide variety of events ranging from England's 1966 World Cup triumph against West Germany to the place where Pope John Paul celebrated a Mass in 1982. However, its poor facilities, coupled with its inaccessible location, led to calls for Wembley to be closed and a new national stadium built in a more central location. Despite various suggestions for alternative locations, in the end the Football Association decided Wembley was the most desirable venue for corporate clients and in 2002 the decision was taken to build a new Wembley Stadium on the grounds of the old one. The Old Wembley was finally closed in 2000 and the twin towers came down in December 2002.

GROUND: **Wembley Stadium**
ADDRESS: Wembley stadium, Wembley Way, London HA9 0WS
CAPACITY: 85,500
PITCH DIMENSIONS: 105m x 68m (115 x 74 yards)
OPENED: 1923
CLOSED: 2000
RECORD ATTENDANCE: 126,047

Plans for a new national stadium were drawn up in the 1990s after the facilities at Old Wembley were deemed inadequate for the modern game. The old Wembley stadium was demolished in 2002, and shortly afterwards the construction of a new Wembley Stadium began. The 90,000-seater stadium will primarily stage football, rugby and music events, but it will also be a venue for major athletics meetings. To turn the stadium into an athletics venue there is a removable steel and concrete platform, 6m above the football pitch, with a 400m

READING

Reading FC was formed in 1871, and played their early games at five different grounds before finally moving to Elm Park in 1894, where they would remain for 104 years. The first job for the club was to level out the sloping pitch. The ground opened in 1896, and had turfed terraces around the pitch and a single wooden Main Stand on the Norfolk Road side. The club built an L-shaped terrace cover over the north-west corner, although this was blown down in a gale in 1925, as was the Main Stand. In 1926 Reading were preparing to play in the Second Division and so decided to build a new Main Stand. The following year saw Elm Park attract its highest capacity ever, with 33,042 packing in to see a Cup tie against Brentford. A roof was added to the South Bank in 1936, which was extended to cover the Town End and the Tilehurst End by the mid 1950s. Few major developments took place until a suggestion in 1983 that Reading and Oxford should merge. This shook the club to its foundations; the club was flailing in the Fourth Division and was attracting crowds of less than 4,000. A new chairman, Roger Smee, took over and turned Reading's fortunes around. Despite improving the ground, Smee had already drawn up plans to move the club to a new site, close to the M4. There was widespread support for the plans, but there was not the cash available to make them a reality. Roger Smee stepped down as chairman in 1990, and Reading was taken over by millionaire publisher John Madejski. He saw Reading promoted to the First Division and pushed the plans forward for a move to the M4 site. Reading played their final game at Elm Park in 1998. The new stadium, the Madejski Stadium, is a 24,200 all-seater stadium, purpose-built for the club. It opened at the start of the 1998 season and is totally enclosed on all sides. There are three single-tiered stands and a two-tiered West Stand.

GROUND: **Madejski Stadium**
ADDRESS: **Madejski Stadium, Bennet Road, Reading, Becks, RG2 OFL**
MAIN TEL: **0118 968 1100**
BOX OFFICE: **0118 968 1000**
WEBSITE: **www.readingfc.co.uk**
CAPACITY: **24,200**
HOME COLOURS: **Royal blue and white hooped shirts, blue shorts, blue socks with white hoops**
CLUB NICKNAME: **The Royals**
PITCH DIMENSIONS: **102m x 70m (112 x 64 yards)**
FOUNDED: **1871**
RECORD ATTENDANCE: **33,042 vs Brentford February 19 1927**
MOST PROLIFIC SCORER: **Ronnie Blackman (158)**
RECORD WIN: **10-2 vs Crystal Palace September 4 1946**
RECORD DEFEAT: **0-18 vs Preston North End January 27 1893**

SHEFFIELD UNITED

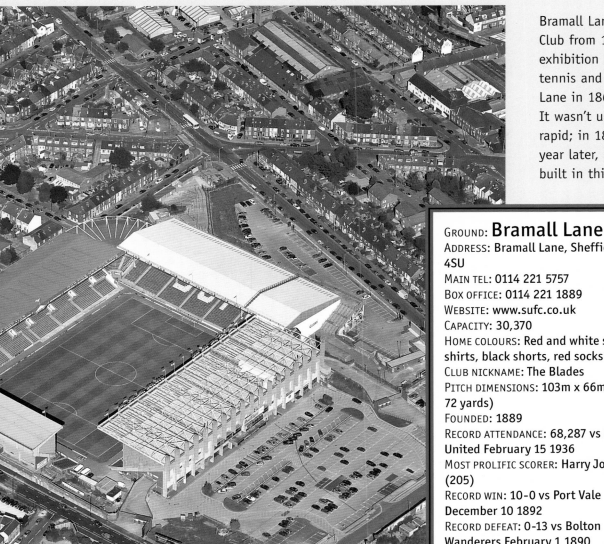

Bramall Lane was originally used as a cricket ground by Sheffield United Cricket Club from 1854. The ground was used for various sporting activities; in 1874 an exhibition baseball match was played at Bramall Lane; bowls, lacrosse, cycling, tennis and athletics were also played there. Football was first played at Bramall Lane in 1862 when Hallam FC took on Sheffield FC, the world's oldest football club. It wasn't until 1889 that Sheffield United Football Club was formed. Success was rapid; in 1892 they were elected to the Second Division, earning promotion just a year later, and winning their only league championship in 1898. Two stands were built in this time, at the Shoreham Street End and on John Street. Glaswegian engineers were behind the 1902 design of the John Street Stand, replacing the earlier one that had been gutted by fire. The Blades won the FA Cup that season, for the second time in their history. Just before the First World War terracing was extended along the Bramall Lane End, known to fans as the Kop. A roof was added in 1935, and just a year later Bramall Lane notched up its highest attendance ever, with 68,287 fans (many of whom sat on the roof) cramming in to see the Blades take on Leeds United. Bramall Lane was bombed 10 times during the war, damaging the John Street stand, the Kop roof and the pitch. It took until 1954 to replace the John Street stand. The South Stand opened in 1975, at a cost of £1m. The ground had a capacity of 49,000, yet the club's fortunes were faltering. By 1981, the Blades were in the fourth division with gates of fewer than 15,000. The 1990s saw a new owner, and further development of the ground. The John Street Stand was demolished in 1994 and a new stand opened in 1996; two of the ground's corners have now been filled bringing the capacity up to 32,000.

GROUND: **Bramall Lane**
ADDRESS: **Bramall Lane, Sheffield S2 4SU**
MAIN TEL: **0114 221 5757**
BOX OFFICE: **0114 221 1889**
WEBSITE: **www.sufc.co.uk**
CAPACITY: **30,370**
HOME COLOURS: **Red and white striped shirts, black shorts, red socks**
CLUB NICKNAME: **The Blades**
PITCH DIMENSIONS: **103m x 66m (112 x 72 yards)**
FOUNDED: **1889**
RECORD ATTENDANCE: **68,287 vs Leeds United February 15 1936**
MOST PROLIFIC SCORER: **Harry Johnson (205)**
RECORD WIN: **10-0 vs Port Vale December 10 1892**
RECORD DEFEAT: **0-13 vs Bolton Wanderers February 1 1890**

SHEFFIELD WEDNESDAY

GROUND: Hillsborough
ADDRESS: Hillsborough, Sheffield S6 1SW
MAIN TEL: 0114 221 2121
BOX OFFICE: 0114 221 2400
WEBSITE: www.swfc.co.uk
CAPACITY: 39,859
HOME COLOURS: Blue and white striped shirts, black shorts, black socks
CLUB NICKNAME: The Owls
PITCH DIMENSIONS: 105m x 68m (115 x 74 yards)
FOUNDED: 1867
RECORD ATTENDANCE: 72,841 vs Manchester City February 17 1934
MOST PROLIFIC SCORER: Andy Wilson (199)
RECORD WIN: 12-0 vs Halliwell January 17 1891
RECORD DEFEAT: 0-10 vs Aston Villa October 5 1912

Sheffield Wednesday was established in 1867 as the footballing element of Wednesday Cricket Club. The club played at various grounds before moving to Olive Grove in 1887. By then they had severed ties with the cricket club. In 1892 the club joined the League and in 1896 they won the FA Cup, which financed the build of a Main Stand. The lease to the ground came up in 1898 and Wednesday found themselves homeless. The crowd were invited to help select a new ground, but in the event none of the selected grounds were suitable and in 1899 the club moved to a ground in Owlerton. The club transported the Main Stand from the Olive Ground to the Owlerton ground, and the new ground brought the club good luck; in 1903 and 1904 they won the League title and in 1907 they won the FA Cup again. It wasn't until 1913 that further developments took place, with a Spion Kop and a South Stand being built. The club changed the ground's name to Hillsborough in 1914, and when the Kop finally opened later that year the capacity was 50,000. In 1927 the Leppings Lane End was expanded, and by 1934 a record 72,841 fans packed in to see the Owls take on Manchester City. A cantilevered grandstand, the North Stand, capable of seating 9,882 fans, replaced the Olive Grove Stand in 1961. Hillsborough was selected as a venue for some of the games in the 1966 World Cup, so Wednesday built a new West Stand and added seats to the South Stand paddock. On April 15 1989 the ground saw its darkest day when 96 Liverpool fans were crushed to death in the Leppings Lane end. This event changed the future of British football, as the resulting Taylor report required all top division clubs in England, Wales and Scotland to become all-seater by the start of the 1994 season. The Owls spent £10m on ground improvements, adding seats to the South Stand, the lower tier of the West Stand and the Kop. The ground can now hold 39,859.

GROUND: **Wembley Stadium**
ADDRESS: **Wembley Stadium**
MAIN TEL: **020 8795 9000**
BOX OFFICE: **0845 676 2006**
WEBSITE: **www.wembleystadium.com**
CAPACITY: **90,000**
PITCH DIMENSIONS: **105m x 68m (115 x 74 yards)**

running track. The most unusual feature of the new stadium, however, is its arch – a 133m tall structure located above the north stand. Made of steel, the arch is 315m long and is the longest single roof structure in the world. The arch supports all of the weight of the north roof as well as some of the south. It sits at an angle of 68° from the horizontal. It is this feature which enables the roof to slide back to let light on to the pitch. The arch was lifted into place in June 2004. It towers 133m (436ft) above the level of the external concourse and it is estimated that the London Eye could sit comfortably between the pitch and the top of the arch. The

all-seater stands have been designed in a bowl shape and, with 90,000 seats, the stadium will be the largest football stadium in the world where every seat is under cover. No seat will have an obstructed view and the legroom in each seat is larger than that enjoyed in the royal box in the Old Wembley stadium. The circumference of the stadium measures one kilometre. The stadium boasts many state of the art facilities, including two giant screens, each the size of 600 domestic television sets, escalators totalling 400m (1312ft) in length as well as 2,618 toilets. The new ground has cost an estimated £760m to develop.

WEST BROMWICH ALBION

West Bromwich Albion FC was created by a group of workers from Salter's Spring Works in 1878. More than 100 years after they formed, they are one of only a few English football clubs to have won all three major honours – the League title, the FA Cup and the League Cup. They originally called themselves the West Bromwich Strollers after walking to nearby Wednesbury to buy themselves a ball. The name stuck until 1880, when they changed their name to the more familiar Albion. The club played at five different grounds before settling at the Hawthorns in 1900, so called as the ground was once surrounded by hawthorn bushes. Situated between Birmingham and Sandwell, the initial capacity was 35,500, but when the club bought the ground's freehold in 1913, it began developing the stands. Concrete terracing was installed in 1920, and by 1924 the capacity reached 65,000. Terracing was completed on all four sides of the ground in 1931, the year the club won the FA Cup for the third time and promotion to division one. In 1937 the club's record attendance of 64,815 watched the Baggies take on Arsenal in the sixth round of the FA Cup. The more familiar stands were built between the 1940s and the 1960s. The East Stand, known as the Rainbow Stand because of its multi-coloured seats, was built on the site of the former Handsworth Stand. Improvements continued to the Birmingham Road End, which was covered in 1964, and the Halfords Lane side. The 1960s also saw the emergence of the Baggies' two most prolific scorers, Jeff Astle and Tony Brown. Following the Taylor report, a £4.15m all-seater stadium was opened in 1995. The Rainbow Stand was finally demolished in 2001 to make way for the new East Stand. When it opened in 2002 to a 1-0 defeat by Grimsby, the Hawthorns became fully functional.

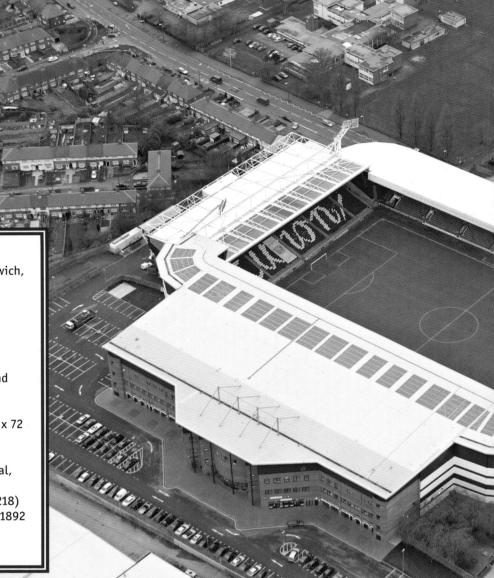

GROUND: **The Hawthorns**
ADDRESS: **Halfords Lane, West Bromwich, West Midlands, B71 4LF**
MAIN TEL: **0121 525 8888**
BOX OFFICE: **0121 525 8888**
WEBSITE: **www.wba.co.uk**
CAPACITY: **28,003**
HOME COLOURS: **Navy blue and white striped shirts, white shorts, blue and white socks**
CLUB NICKNAME: **The Baggies**
PITCH DIMENSIONS: **105m x 66m (115 x 72 yards)**
FOUNDED: **1878**
RECORD ATTENDANCE: **64,815 vs Arsenal, March 6 1937**
MOST PROLIFIC SCORER: **Tony Brown (218)**
RECORD WIN: **12-0 vs Darwen April 4 1892**
RECORD DEFEAT: **3-10 vs Stoke City February 4 1937**

WEST HA

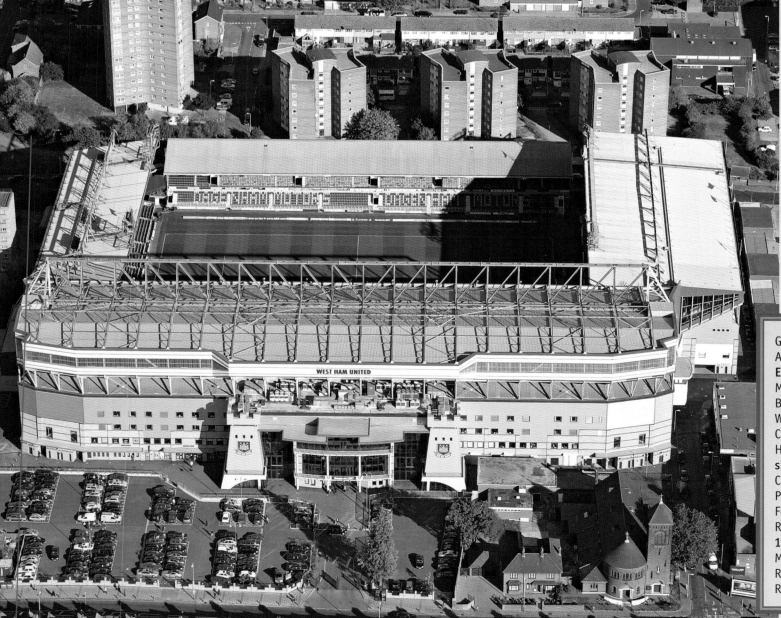

West Ham United started out as Thames Ironworks, a team set up by Arnold Hills in 1895. Hills was a shipyard owner, and the nickname "the Hammers" refers to the tools of shipyard workers. The team originally played at Hermit Road in Canning Town before eventually moving to Upton Park in 1904, four years after renaming themselves West Ham United. The club's ground is actually called the Boleyn Ground, named after a 16th-century house that

GROUND: **Upton Park**
ADDRESS: **Boleyn Ground, Green Street, Upton Park, London E13 9AZ**
MAIN TEL: **020 8548 2748**
BOX OFFICE: **020 8548 2700**
WEBSITE: **www.whufc.com**
CAPACITY: **35,640**
HOME COLOURS: **Claret shirts with blue sleeves, white shorts, light blue socks with claret hoops**
CLUB NICKNAME: **The Hammers**
PITCH DIMENSIONS: **110m x 64m (112 x 72 yards)**
FOUNDED: **1895**
RECORD ATTENDANCE: **42,322 vs Tottenham Hotspur October 17 1970**
MOST PROLIFIC SCORER: **Vic Watson (306)**
RECORD WIN: **8-0 vs Sunderland October 19 1968**
RECORD DEFEAT: **2-8 vs Blackburn Rovers December 26 1963**

WIGAN ATHLETIC

Springfield Park, Wigan's original home ground, was first used for football in 1897 by Wigan County. Before then the ground was a sports ground, with a horse trotting track, a concrete cycle track and a running track. Following Wigan County's demise, a succession of Wigan clubs formed and disbanded, with Wigan Borough being the most successful, lasting from 1919 to 1932. During Borough's ownership of the ground the original stands were replaced and a new main stand created. The Shevington End Stand and the Popular Side stand were also constructed during this period. When Wigan Athletic formed in 1932, they bought Springfield Park and this would be home to the Latics for the next 67 years. The Latics' first game at Springfield Park was against Port Vale Reserves, which ended in a 2-0 defeat for the home side.

The club fought for football league status until 1978. During this time the club drew the largest crowd in its history. More than 27,500 fans turned up to see the Latics beat Hereford United 4-1 in the third round of the FA Cup and draw with Newcastle United in the next round. The Latics finally made it to the football league after 34 attempts in 1978. They marked the occasion by losing 3-0 to Grimsby Town. The Latics had mixed success after joining the league. An impressive start saw them promoted to the third division at the end of the 1981-82 season. They stared bankruptcy and relegation to the Conference in the face after a bad run of results in the 1992-3 season, but their fortunes were reversed when local businessman Dave Whelan bought the club in 1995. He subsidised the building of a new stadium, the JJB stadium, which they moved to in 1999. The new stadium is shared with local rugby league team Wigan Warriors.

GROUND: **JJB Stadium**
ADDRESS: **Loire Drive, Wigan, WN5 0UZ**
MAIN TEL: **01942 244433**
BOX OFFICE: **01942 244433**
WEBSITE: **www.wiganlatics.com**
CAPACITY: **25,000**
HOME COLOURS: **Blue with white and green**
CLUB NICKNAME: **The Latics**
PITCH DIMENSIONS: **110m x 60m (120 x 66 yards)**
FOUNDED: **1932**
RECORD ATTENDANCE: **27,526 (vs Hereford United 12 March 1953)**
MOST PROLIFIC SCORER: **Peter Houghton (62 goals)**
RECORD WIN: **7-1 vs Scarborough March 1997**
RECORD DEFEAT: **1-6 vs Bristol Rovers March 1990**

M UNITED

stood next door to the ground. The club proved popular and in 1913 a new West Stand was built, which was extended in 1925 to a two-tier structure. During this time the South Stand was covered, as was the East Stand. The Second World War saw severe damage to the South Stand when a V1 bomb landed on the ground. The 1960s brought sweeping changes to Upton Park, beginning with the covering of the North Bank. Another bay was added to the West Stand and the East Stand was completely rebuilt, significantly raising Upton Park's capacity, so much so that a record 42,322 fans saw the Hammers take on Spurs in a First Division derby in 1970. As with many other clubs, the ground had to reduce its capacity following the Taylor report. In 1991, the club bought land behind the West Stand, which they rebuilt and expanded. However, the club was in financial difficulties, and in November 1991 it came up with a disastrous bond scheme. Boycotts and pitch protests followed and gates dropped below 16,000. To try and lure fans back, the club slashed the price of season tickets, and eventually began redeveloping the South Stand (now the Centenary Stand) in 1993. The Bobby Moore Stand opened in 1994 and the millennium brought further redevelopments to the West and East Stands, raising the capacity of the ground to 35,640.

WOLVERHAMPTON WANDERERS

Wolves formed from a schoolboys' team, St Lukes, in 1877, which then merged with a local cricket and football team in 1879 to form Wolverhampton Wanderers. After playing home games at Goldthorn Hill and Dudley Road, the club moved to Molineux in 1889. Molineux had been long used for sporting events before being taken over by Wolves. A grandstand was built which could seat 300 spectators, and there was shelter for a further 4,000 fans. Wolves played their first League game in 1889 against Notts County, which they won 2-0. Despite boasting a capacity of 20,000, it was not until 1925 that the major stands were built. The first was erected on the Waterloo Road side of the ground. The Molineux Street stand was rebuilt in 1932 after a gale blew the old cover down. This distinctive structure had a multi-span roof, with a clock mounted in the centre. The 1930s saw the north and south end terracing covered to shelter the large crowds that flocked to home games. During this period, 61,315 fans turned up to see Wolves take on Liverpool, the largest crowd ever recorded. During the 1950s, Molineux was best known for its newly installed floodlights. Top European clubs flocked to the Midlands ground to enjoy the opportunities of midweek evening games that floodlights made possible. In 1978, new legislation led to the demolition of the Molineux Street stand and, in its place, a £2m grandstand was erected. This stand almost led to the club folding as they struggled to cope with the debt, but in 1986 they were saved by the local council who bought the ground for £1.12m. In May 1990 Sir Jack Hayward purchased Molineux for an estimated £20m, redeveloping the ground into one of the then most modern in the country.

GROUND: **Molineux**
ADDRESS: **Molineux Ground, Waterloo Road, Wolverhampton WV1 4QR**
MAIN TEL: **01902 655 000**
BOX OFFICE: **0870 442 0123**
WEBSITE: **www.wolves.co.uk**
CAPACITY: **28,500**
HOME COLOURS: **Gold shirts, black shorts**
CLUB NICKNAME: **Wolves**
PITCH DIMENSIONS: **101m x 69m (110 x 75yards)**
FOUNDED: **1877**
RECORD ATTENDANCE: **61,315 vs Liverpool February 11 1939 FA Cup 5th Round**
MOST PROLIFIC SCORER: **Steve Bull (247)**
RECORD WIN: **10-1 vs Leicester City April 15 1938**
RECORD DEFEAT: **1-10 vs Newton Heath 15 October 1892**

"Your Stadium" was created to provide you, the fan, with a fun and unique view of your favourite football stadiums around the country. We've also included the National Stadiums and many major grounds from around the world. The grounds can be downloaded and printed onto photographic paper as posters or used as screen savers.

Visit yourstadium.com

First published in 2005 by
Myriad Books Limited
35 Bishopsthorpe Road, London SE26 4PA

Photographs © Flight Images

Text copyright © Cassandra Wells

Cassandra Wells has asserted her right under the Copyright, Designs and Patents Act 1998 to be identified as the author of this work.

ISBN 1 904 736 00 9

Designed by Jerry Goldie Graphic Design

Printed in China

www.myriadbooks.com